GREAT AMERICAN RAILROADS

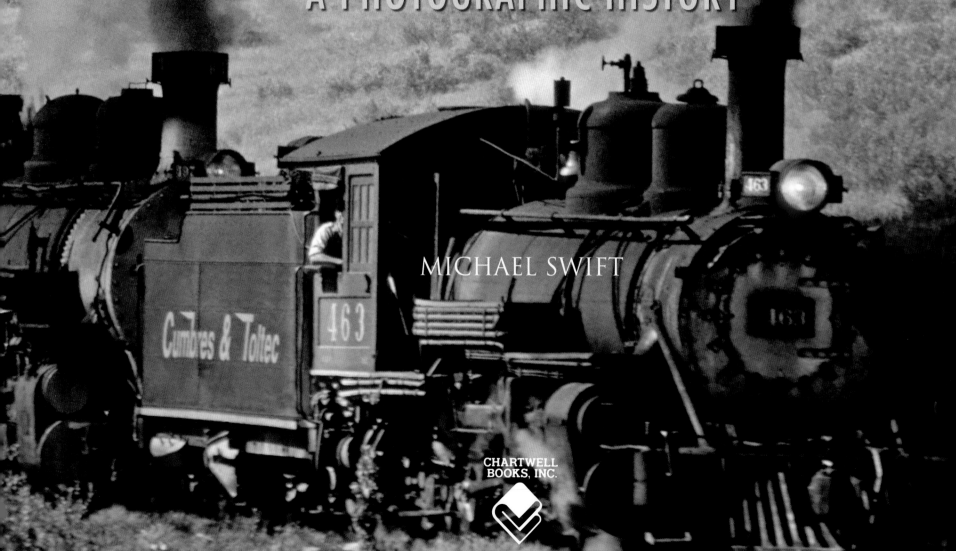

GREAT AMERICAN RAILROADS

A PHOTOGRAPHIC HISTORY

MICHAEL SWIFT

CHARTWELL
BOOKS, INC.

This edition published in 2013 by
CHARTWELL BOOKS, INC.
A division of BOOK SALES, INC.
276 Fifth Avenue Suite 206
New York, New York 10001
USA

This edition published by arrangement with
Compendium Publishing Limited.

Editor: Don Gulbrandsen
Design: Danny Gillespie

ISBN-13: 978-0-7858-2960-7

Printed and bound in China

10 9 8 7 6 5 4 3 2 1

PAGE 1: Grand Canyon Poster by Oscar Bryn.
Swim Ink 2, LLC/Corbis

PAGE 3: Triple-headed steam on the Cumbres &
Toltec Scenic Railroad. *Aurora/Getty Images*

RIGHT: Locos UP5050, UP9848, UP9069, and
UP4261 depart from Tunnel 5 at Bealville (between
Bakersfield and Mojave) wth a southbound stack
train from Oakland to Chicago, September 20,
2003. *Colin J. Marsden*

CONTENTS

Introduction

Railroads changed the face of the world. They revolutionized the bulk transit of goods and people, allowing industry to blossom by bringing raw materials and workers to where they were needed. Rail travel also revolutionized concepts of personal mobility, allowing the individual the chance of traveling further faster than before. Within a hundred years of its invention, rail travel was possible on nearly a million miles of track worldwide.

Nowhere was this more true than in the United States where railroads had their most dramatic growth: by 1840 more than 3,000 miles of railroad were already operating in the eastern states, a figure 40 percent greater than the total railroad mileage of Europe. By the eve of the Civil War, the iron network in the United States was more than 30,000 mile long, and railroads had nearly caught up with the ever-moving western frontier. By 1860 the railroad had clearly shown its superiority over turnpikes, canals, and steamboats. Following the Civil War, several lines were extended all the way to the Pacific coast, the first being the Union Pacific-Central Pacific, completed in 1869. By 1890 the length of the U.S. rail system was 163,000 miles; by 1916 it had reached an all-time high of 254,000 miles. In Canada the first rail service started in 1836 and by 1880 the network had expanded to about 6,960 miles. The Canadian Pacific Railway was completed across the Rockies to the Pacific by 1885.

In the rush to be first, many railroads went broke due to the huge investment needed to create them and their immense running costs. The Erie Railroad, the Northern Pacific, and the Atchison, Topeka & Santa Fe all went bankrupt in 1893. The stakes were high and business was cutthroat: ticket prices were slashed to undercut the competition; railroads went on different tracks to the same destinations, and a vast amount of stock was sold. It couldn't last; reason finally prevailed. By 1900 amalgamation had produced six distinct systems that worked hard to create sensible timetables and charge realistic fares. America at last had a railroad network to be proud of. But with the advent of the combustion engine the golden age of the railroad was over even before the start of the 1920s.

How quickly things change! Today in the U.S. not only has steam disappeared, but the train, too, has lost much of its appeal to passengers. Cheap, efficient, uncomplicated internal air routes and the explosion of car ownership rendered many

of the unique properties of railways no longer necessary features of the modern world. For freight, however, the railroads remain essential; while most of the great names of U.S. railroading no longer run long-distance passenger services—Amtrak having assumed this responsibility in the early 1970s—freight continues to travel in vast quantities across the nation in massive trains.

But as they disappeared, people began to realize that there was more to the railroad than just an inefficient old passenger system: the great locomotives were awesome, powerful behemoths that came alive when they ran, belching smoke and steam, and sparks. People began to preserve these mechanical marvels and buy up stretches of line to run them on. Pretty soon, this preservation movement, which had started as a labor of love, became a part of the tourist industry and now the wheel has turned full circle. Railroads have become good business again—but as tourist and scenic lines rather than essential parts of the country's economic fabric.

LEFT: The world's first preserved standard-gauge railroad was the Strasburg Railroad in Pennsylvania. *H. Bongaardt*

BELOW: Demonstrating where the profits on U.S. railroads come from—freight trains from Burlington Northern Santa Fe (BNSF) and Union Pacific run parallel to each other, June 4, 2004. *Colin J. Marsden*

Railroad History

As in Europe and in particular Great Britain, the first railroads in the U.S. grew up to serve industry in the years before the arrival of public railroads. The generally accepted first public railroad in the U.S. was the Baltimore & Ohio (although there were earlier lines, such as the Granite Railway at Quincy in Boston constructed in 1826 for work on the Bunker Hill memorial, these were not "public" in the sense of offering a public service), which was first launched at a meeting of Baltimore businessmen in 1827 and, despite opposition from powerful forces, including Congress, work started on July 4, 1828, and the first thirteen-mile section opened in May 1830. The railroad was initially horse-powered, but in August 1830 the first steam locomotive operated over the line. This was Peter Cooper's *Tom Thumb* but this locomotive was not the first in the U.S. The honor of being the first steam locomotive in North America belonged to an imported locomotive from Britain—the *Stourbridge Lion*—which had been tested on the Delaware & Hudson Canal & Railroad but which had been deemed unsuitable by the company's engineer, Horatio Allen.

The first successful steam-operated railroad, however, was probably the South Carolina Railroad, which inaugurated its services on December 25, 1830, using the vertical-boilered *Best Friend of Charleston*. The locomotive subsequently suffered a burst boiler as a result of a problem with its safety valve, but steam traction had well and truly arrived in the U.S. At this date there were only some twenty-three miles of operational railroad track in the U.S. of which thirteen miles was represented by the Baltimore & Ohio. However, once the principal of the steam-hauled railway was established, expansion was paid. Within five years of the opening of the B&O total mileage in the U.S. reached more than 1,000 miles and this total almost tripled by 1840 when some 2,800 route miles was in operation. By the end of the 1840s, a total of some 9,000 miles of track had been, although the bulk—some two-thirds—was located in eleven Mid-Atlantic and New England states (New York, with some 1,361 route miles possessed the most intensive network in 1850).

Alongside the growth in the network during these early years there was also rapid development in the locomotives and rolling stock used by the railways. Initially, most of the steam engines constructed for use on U.S. railroads were designed to be

Built by the West Point Foundry in New York, *De Witt Clinton* first operated over the South Carolina Railroad on August 9, 1831. It, too, survived to appear at the Chicago Exhibition of 1893. *Ian Allan Library*

fueled by wood, of which the country had an abundance; however, coal was gradually adopted as an alternative. Unfortunately, the most readily available coal was of the hard anthracite variety, which proved difficult to burn in the small fireboxes of the day. This problem resulted in some of the more unusual designs to emerge during these early years. The early coal-burning locomotives were fitted with vertical, as opposed to the more usual horizontal boilers; as a result of their peculiar shape and motion, these locomotives were nicknamed "Grasshoppers" or "Crabs." These locomotives, however, ran slowly and needed more work. Ross Winans developed an alternative design, with an enlarged firebox and the cab located above the boiler; these locomotives—nicknamed for obvious reasons—"Camels," first appeared in 1848 and this design was to be further refined later in the 19th century as "Camelbacks" (or "Mother Hubbards").

Parallel to these developments, there were also advances in the more common wood-burning locomotive, most notably in the late 1830s when the Philadelphia-based Norris company produced its first 4-4-0 design; first constructed in 1837, the 4-4-0 was probably the archetypal U.S. steam locomotive of these early years and was undoubtedly the design that enabled the railroad frontier to be driven ever westwards. The huge domestic demand plus the ever-increasing need for more powerful locomotives ensured that the U.S. was at the forefront of steam locomotive development right through to the middle of the twentieth century. It was no coincidence that it was the U.S. that pioneered the development of designs such as the Atlantic (4-4-2) and Pacific (4-6-2) wheel arrangements that were ultimately to become dominant through much of the world. But locomotive development in the U.S. did not stop there; it ran through to the massive 4-8-8-4 "Big Boys" and similar massive machines of the 1930s and 1940s. Moreover, manufacturers such as the American Locomotive Company (Alco) and Baldwin manufactured locomotives in massive numbers both for the domestic and export markets.

Passenger accommodation also developed during these years. The early railroad coaches had been little more than stagecoaches fitted with flanged wheels. Within a few years passenger cars had grown in scale becoming, in the words of English actress Fanny Kemble who lived in the U.S. for a number of years after moving there in 1832 "a long greenhouse on wheels."

During the 1850s the U.S. railroad network again expand threefold, reaching a total mileage of some 30,000 on the eve of the Civil War. Railroads, however, remained largely an East Coast phenomenon. This was inevitable, however, given the population and economic development of this region and the fact that the western border of the country was only gradually extending toward the Pacific. The discovery of gold in California was, however, the spur that was required to drive development ever westwards. The 1850s witnessed the construction of a number of highly significant routes. These included the westward extensions of the New York Central

and Erie to Lake Erie and the B&O and Pennsylvania Railroad up the Ohio Valley. At the same time massive development in the states of Illinois, Indiana, and Ohio saw route mileage in those three states increase tenfold to some 11,000 miles in total.

Although many of the lines constructed were built to the accepted standard gauge of 4 feet 8.5 inches, this was not uniform. The Erie, for example, was constructed to a gauge of 6 feet 0 inches and many of the lines in Ohio, for example, were built to a gauge of 4 feet 10 inches. While the network was relatively fragmented this did not prove a serious handicap but once problems of transhipment and interchange of rolling stock occurred, the differences in gauge proved a barrier. It was not, however, until the 1880s that 4 feet 8.5 inches became the accepted national standard; the last southern routes were converted on June 1, 1886. Some narrow-gauge lines were also constructed, but these were only of relatively limited importance.

However, the early years of the 1860s were to witness the first major war in the world where the railroad was to play a significant part. Both the Confederate and Union forces made considerable use of railroads for the movement of men and materiel; in the autumn of 1863, for example, 30,000 Union troops were moved by rail in order to help relieve Chattanooga, Tennessee, which was then under Confederate siege. Railroads allowed for the rapid movement of men and

equipment much more quickly and in much greater quantities than before. As both sides realized the potential for railroads, they also realized that destroying the enemy's lines of communication would aid their own campaign and the war was thus to witness considerable destruction. By the end of the war, the country's railroads were near to collapse but it would not be long before they were restored and expansion could continue apace.

Once peace had been restored and the wartime damage repaired, the westward march of the Union could continue and as the country expanded westwards the railroad followed. The next 50 years were to see a further massive development in the country's railroad infrastructure symbolized, perhaps, by that moment on May 10, 1869, when the golden spike was inserted at Promontory Point, Utah, between the Union Pacific and Central Pacific railroads to mark the completion of the first transcontinental railroad. Between 1870 and the turn of the century a further four routes would be completed across the continent: the Southern Pacific from California to New Orleans; the Santa Fe from Kansas to California; the Northern Pacific from Minnesota to Seattle; and the Great Northern, which also linked the upper Midwest and the Pacific Northwest. Between 1865, when the Civil War concluded, and 1916, on the eve of the U.S.'s entry into World War I, total route mileage in the country increased from some 30,000 miles to a massive 254,000 miles.

LEFT: A number of early steam locomotives operated in the U.S. were imported from Great Britain. One such example was *John Bull*, a locomotive constructed in Britain in 1831 and operated by the Camden & Ambor Railroad (later part of the Pennsylvania Railroad). The locomotive was retired in 1865 and passed to the Smithsonian Institution but was to operate again, as shown here, with two coaches at the 1893 World's Columbia Exhibition at Chicago. Still part of the Smithsonian's collection, the locomotive is the oldest surviving original engine in the U.S. *Ian Allan Library*

One of the B&O's early vertical-boilered coal-powered steam engines; these were designed to compensate for problems caused by the use of anthracite but were not developed any further. *Ian Allan Library*

One factor that stimulated much of this railway development was the grant of land. In 1850 legislation proposed by senators William King and Stephen Douglas allowed for the granting of land to the Illinois-Central-Mobile & Ohio route to the Gulf of Mexico. After the Civil War, 80 different lines received land grants, totalling some 131 million acres, and some 40 percent of the railroad track constructed in the west by 1880 had been built with the aid of these land grants. There was a downside, however, to the receipt of these grants; those railroads that received land grants had to give 50 percent discount on rates for all federal or government traffic.

Alongside all the growth in the U.S. railroad industry prior to 1914 there was a further downside: corruption. Wherever money was to be found there would be those that would seek to make their share of it either legally or illegally and, given the sheer scale of the railroading industry prior to the outbreak of World War I, it was not surprising that there were those that were accused of financial chicanery. Figures such as Cornelius Vanderbilt of the New York Central was both a victim and a perpetrator as he sought to manipulate the company's shares; it was perhaps appropriate that his staff nicknamed the company's all-black locomotives "Black Crooks." Corruption came in many forms; share manipulation was only one aspect. In 1872, for example, the Crédit Mobilier scandal hit the Union Pacific when it was discovered that up to $23 million had been paid out dishonestly to insiders. Crédit Mobilier was one of the major construction companies involved in the building of the line and it had made illicit payments to senior officers of the railroad. It was not alone; similar scandals affected other railroads as well.

Corruption was not the only problem to afflict the railroad industry prior to the war. Lack of competition, particularly in areas like the Midwest, sometimes led to unreasonably high prices for rail transportation. Farmers were among those most severely affected by the high costs and, in 1867, a new organization—the National Grange of the Patrons of Husbandry—was established to fight for farmers' rights. This organization was initially designed to act primarily for educational and social purposes, but soon became a forum for political action. Inspired by the NGPH, various Midwestern states, such as Illinois, Iowa, Minnesota, and Wisconsin, introduced Granger Laws in the years after 1870 regulating the freight rates that the railroads could charge. However, while the Supreme Court ruled that individual states could legislate on freight rates, the Wabash case of 1886 confirmed that a state could not regulate freight passing from one state to another; this would require action by the Federal government. The result was the Interstate Commerce Act of 1886, which established the Interstate Commerce Commission; this was the first piece of government legislation to regulate the railroad industry. Although it established a principle, the new act was not a great success with only one decision going against the railroads out of sixteen cases brought between 1887 and 1905. Federal regulation of railroads was further strengthened by the Elkins Act (1903), the Hepburn Act (1906),

and the Mann-Elkins Act (1910). These acts considerably enhanced the powers of the ICC and saw the end of the practice of offering rebates, for example, and allowed for the right to establish freight rates that were "just and reasonable."

The last decades of the nineteenth century were not, however, wholly without positive developments. There were significant improvements in the design of steam locomotives, which got larger and more powerful. It was not only in steam traction that progress was made; towards the end of the nineteenth century electric traction first made its appearance. The principle of using electricity to power a locomotive had been established at the Berlin Exhibition of 1879 and, in 1895 the B&O became the first railroad in the U.S. to adopt this means of traction when it electrified 3.25 miles of track to its Baltimore Mount Royal station. An ordinance had banned the use of steam within the city's boundaries and so, until the adoption of electricity, the B&O had been forced to use horse power within the city. In New York the city, concerned about pollution, banned steam south of the Harlem River in 1908, thus forcing the New York Central to electrify its line between Grand Central and Croton using the third-rail principle.

There were also developments in freight cars with the first refrigerated cars for perishable produce appearing in 1867, the first horizontal tank cars in 1868 and vastly improved livestock cars in the 1880s. The size of cars also increased. An ore hopper, for example, in the 1860s had a capacity of some 10 tons; by the outbreak of World War I this had increased to some 40 tons. The more powerful locomotives and the larger cars allowed for longer and heavier trains; between 1870 and 1915, for example, freight train weights on the Illinois Central rose more than five-fold. Passenger stock also improved considerably during these years as passengers demanded faster trains and more comfortable accommodation. At the forefront of these developments was George Pullman, whose name became synonymous with luxury travel. He pioneered the provision of dining cars on trains while other improvements saw better heating and the use of electric, rather than gas or oil, lighting. There were also developments in terms of better brakes—the air brake developed by George Westinghouse first appeared in the late 1860s—and couplings. Legislation in 1893 made the use of these technical developments standard.

Apart from improvements to their own equipment and services, the railroads also had a profound social consequence on the U.S. Until the railway age there was no single standard system of time zones. In an era when communication was relatively slow the fact that neighboring towns and cities had different times was not significant. The creation of a railroad network, with the need for timetables, showed that uniformity was required. While the U.S. was too large to be covered by a single time zone, there was recognition that change needed to come. On November 18, 1883, four standard time zones—based upon the 75th, 90th, 105th and 120th degrees of longitude—were introduced.

In August 1914, World War I started with the German invasion of Belgium; the European powers, and their colonial empires, became locked into a destructive war. The first war to be fought among the hugely industrialized nations, technology was to see conflict spread further afield than in any previous war. While the U.S. was not involved until late 1917, once the country did declare war, the railroad industry played its part. However, the railroads were not in the best condition to assist the war effort. One consequence of the increased legislation of the prewar years had been to reduce the financial viability of many of the lines, a problem compounded by increasing wage rates among railroad employees (for example the Adamson Act of 1916 had brought in an eight-hour working day with no reduction in pay). The consequences of these factors was that there had been little investment in new locomotives and rolling stock, maintenance had been reduced, and almost 20 percent of the railroad mileage was either in or hovering just above bankruptcy.

One of the first actions after the declaration of war in 1917 was the placing of the railroad industry under federal control on December 28, 1917. This allowed the government to operate the network as a single entity, to eliminate wasteful competition, and to allocate resources where they were needed. With William G.

McAdoo as director-general, state control lasted for twenty-six months. However, the railroad companies were not satisfied either by the rent paid by the government for the use of the track and equipment nor by the level of maintenance undertaken during this period. The railroad companies determined that, in the event of a future conflict, such state control should not be permitted again and, during World War II, they achieved this goal. Coordination was ensured—by the creation on December 18, 1941 by President Roosevelt of the Office of Defense Transportation under Joseph Eastman—but the railroads themselves maintained their own independence.

Following the return of the railroads to private control in early 1920, the industry had a brief period of prosperity before the Great Depression started following the Wall Street Crash of 1929. But the first part of this prosperous period revealed ominous trends regarding the future viability of the railroad industry. World War I had been the first in which road vehicles had played a major role and, in order to provide the vast numbers of trucks and other engines required, a new industry had developed. With the cessation of hostilities, this industry was looking for a new—domestic—market and it was during the early 1920s that mass car ownership first

LEFT: The "Atlantic" locomotive was built by Phineas Davis at York, Pennsylvania, and went into operation on the Baltimore & Ohio Railroad in the summer of 1832. It is shown here pulling two double-deck Imlay coaches. When new, this train was the first to enter Washington, D.C., and led the procession of trains on August 24, 1835. *Underwood & Underwood/Corbis*

started and the rise of the trucking industry also started to pose a threat. By the late 1920s, there were some 23 million private cars on the nation's roads. Both of these developments affected the viability of the railroad industry, a viability further affected by the regulated nature of the railroad industry as opposed to the less stringently controlled road transport industry.

The railroads were forced to respond to these competitive threats. In many parts of the country, passenger services were either significantly reduced or withdrawn completely; it was in 1920, for example, that the Strasburg Railroad (later destined to become the first preserved standard-gauge railroad in the world) lost its passenger services. However, these reductions merely encouraged more people to acquire cars and the vicious circle continued. Takeovers and route rationalization also occurred; between 1916 and 1940, the total rail mileage in the U.S. fell by some 10 percent to 233,000 miles (a decline that has continued since, with mileage falling to less than 200,000 by the mid-1970s). The surviving railroads, however, became more efficient through the use of more powerful locomotives, heavier trains, and significantly fewer personnel. The numbers of workers employed by the railroads fell by a third, to just over one million, between 1916 and 1940.

If the 1930s were a decade of struggle for the railroad industry, they were also years when the industry produced some of the most stylish locomotive designs and services ever witnessed. The era of streamlining was first launched by the Union Pacific's *City of Salina* in 1934. Diesel-powered locomotives, first introduced in the late 1920s, were both cleaner and offered great potential for stylish design, but it was not only the diesel locomotive that achieved streamlining during the 1930s. The passenger steam locomotive, too, saw dramatic designs emerging, for example from New York Central and B&O. The first streamlined steam locomotive was NYC's *Commodore Vanderbilt*, which also debuted in 1934 One of the most influential designers of this period was a French émigré, Raymond Loewy (1893-1986), who fostered a close relationship with the Pennsylvania Railroad, designing both steam and electric locomotives for the company, the last of which were the GG1 electrics that operated until the early 1980s.

While streamlining was undoubtedly dramatic at the time, in terms of the future of U.S. railroads a much more significant development was the creation of the Electro-Motive Division (EMD) of General Motors in 1935, which would ultimately become the largest manufacturer of diesel locomotives in the world. GM had been involved in the development of diesel locomotives since the start of the decade when it acquired it couple of smaller businesses. Early production included work with Union Pacific on its streamlined units, but in 1936, with the opening of a new factory at La Grange, Illinois, production of standardized locomotives commenced. EMD-built locomotives were to become the face of U.S. railroads; even competitors adopted designs similar to those emerging from La Grange. Such

Building the B&O required the construction of a major viaduct at Relay, Maryland. Opened in July 4, 1835, the structure is the oldest stone-arch railway viaduct in the world. This contemporary view, published in Britain, shows a steam train crossing the bridge. *Ian Allan Library*

was EMD's domination that Congress in the mid-1950s investigated the company to see if it was operating an unfair monopoly.

The end of the decade saw Europe enter a world war for the second time in a generation; again the U.S. tried to adopt a policy of neutrality but after the Japanese attack on Pearl Harbor in December 1941 the country was drawn into the conflict. In World War I, when the railroads were taken into state control, there had been an imbalance in traffic as the war was fought almost exclusively in Europe; there were therefore vast shipments of men and equipment from west to east but with little in the return direction. World War II, however, was to be fought both in Europe and in the Pacific, with the consequence that traffic flowed in both directions. Unlike World War I, however, the railroad companies maintained their independence, coordination being achieved by Eastman's Office of Defense Transportation.

In 1946, following the cessation of hostilities, there were 37,500 steam locomotives in operation on U.S. railroads. The last new steam locomotive, constructed for coal-hauler Norfolk & Western, was completed in 1953, but elsewhere steam was in rapid decline. By 1958 the total number of steam locomotives in operation in the U.S. had been reduced to some 1,700 and the final mainline steam locomotives were retired two years later. By this date, however, the first stirrings of the preservation movement had occurred and the first preserved standard-gauge line in the world—at Strasburg, Pennsylvania—had opened in 1959.

Just as the steam locomotive was in decline after the war, so too were many of the railroad finances, particularly when it came to passenger revenue. The rise of the private automobile had already released many from the need to travel by train and this trend was accelerated by the development of the domestic airline business. After all, who'd want to spend nearly a day traveling across the continent when an aircraft could achieve the same in a fraction of the time? There were efforts to try and make passenger trains more cost effective for the operators; in 1949, for example, the Budd Company launched its Rail Diesel Car (RDC). These vehicles, nicknamed "doodlebugs," were self-propelled passenger coaches, designed to operate either singly or in multiple, and undoubtedly the large numbers acquired after 1949 did help sustain many routes for longer than they would have done otherwise. But for the major railroad companies freight traffic was where the profits came from; while the glamorous streamlined expresses may have helped the public profile they did little to satisfy the needs of shareholders and, without the creation of Amtrak in 1970, it is doubtful that long-distance passenger services would have survived in the U.S. As it was, even with the creation of Amtrak, there was a significant reduction in the mileage over which long-distance passenger services operated.

Shorn of their passenger services, but still owning the track and running the freight services, the surviving railroad companies forged ahead. Some prospered; others fell by the wayside. Penn Central—the misbegotten 1968 alliance of eastern

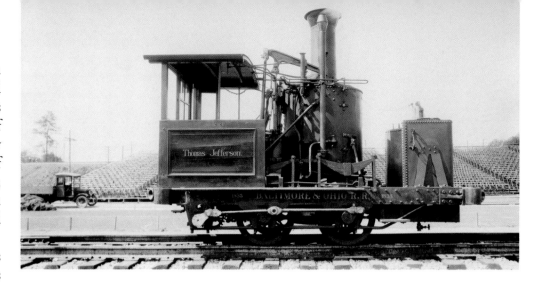

rivals Pennsy and New York Central—for example, fell into the latter category when it failed financially in 1976 and had to replaced by a government-owned corporation, Conrail. Elsewhere, the gradual evolution of the U.S. railroad business by merger and takeover—something that had occurred throughout the history of U.S. railroads—continued apace. Old familiar names disappeared, to be replaced by huge new conglomerates. By the end of the twentieth century, the vast majority of U.S. railroad mileage was in the hands of a small number of companies: CSX; Norfolk Southern; Burlington Northern Santa Fe; Union Pacific; Canadian National; Canadian Pacific; and, Guilford System. Of these only one U.S. railroad name can be said to have survived from the golden age—Union Pacific.

In an age when fuel prices are increasing as resources become scarcer, railroads worldwide are achieving a renaissance. It is an inescapable fact that U.S. railroads also have the potential to play an ever-greater role in the U.S. economy in the future. The investment of more than a century ago, when men literally cut their way through the harsh terrain with pick and shovel, will again prove to have been worthwhile.

LEFT: Another of the early B&O coal-fired vertical-boilered locomotives, *Thomas Jefferson*, which dated from 1836, was the first locomotive owned by the B&O to be fitted with a cab for the locomotive crew and also the first to enter the state of Virginia. These locomotives were nicknamed "grasshoppers." This locomotive remained in service, as a switcher, until 1893. *Ian Allan Library*

BELOW LEFT: Built by H. R. Dunham & Co in 1836 for the 25-mile-long Natchez & Hamburg Railroad in Mississippi, this wood-fired 0-4-0 is now preserved in the Chicago Museum of Science & industry. *Ian Allan Library*

BOTTOM LEFT: Named originally as *Lafeyette* when it entered service, this 4-2-0 was the first parallel-boilered locomotive to enter service with the B&O. It was renamed *William Galloway* for the line's centennial in 1927. *Ian Allan Library*

RIGHT: William Norris of Philadelphia was one of the domestic pioneers of locomotive design in the U.S., working starting the late 1830s. It was Norris who designed the locomotive that could be described as the type that opened up the west—the 4-4-0 design—but Norris Brothers produced a wide variety of designs such as this unusual 6-2-0. *Ian Allan Library*

Built at the Globe Loco Works, Boston, Mass, in 1849 *Pioneer* was brought to California in 1855 — the first locomotive in the state — by ship sailing via Cape Horn. It operated over the Sacramento Valley Railroad until withdrawal in 1888 when it was scrapped. It was the only inside-cylinder locomotive ever to operate on the Pacific coast. *Ian Allan Library*

BELOW: The American Civil War was the first in history where the railroads played a significant role. Here a rudimentary rail-borne howitzer is pictured with canon balls ready to fire. *Corbis*

BELOW RIGHT: Work started on the Hoosac Tunnel in 1851 and continued for nearly a quarter century. When it opened in 1875, it was the longest railroad tunnel in North America—a mark it held until 1928—and the second longest in the world. It provides a link between North Adams and Florida, Massachusetts, and is some 4.75 miles in length. The tunnel, now controlled by the Guilford Rail System, is still used, but for freight trains only. The last regular passenger services ceased in 1958. *Corbis*

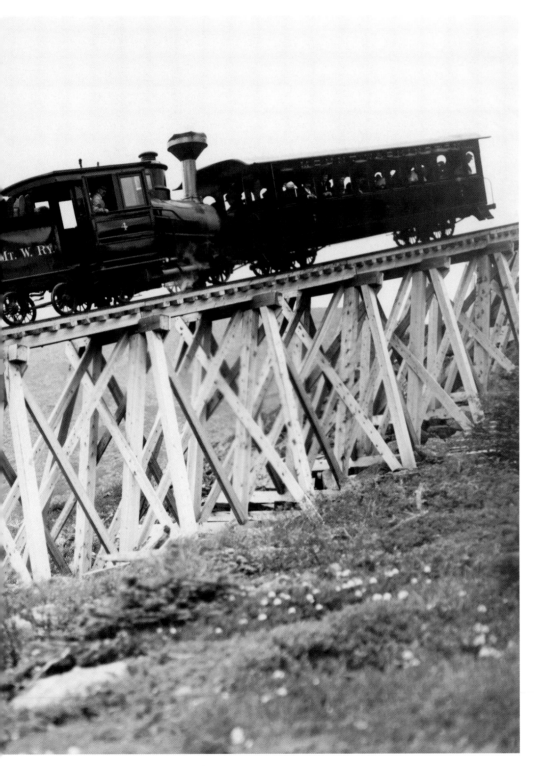

FAR LEFT: Just as the Civil War was the first where armies made significant use of the railways for movement of men and materiel, so too was it the first war where railroads suffered considerable damage as a result of their strategic importance. *Corbis*

ABOVE: One of a pair of stereo images showing bridge construction in 1890, in Minnesota as the Railway of the Pacific gets built. *Roger Viollet/Getty Images*

LEFT: The Mount Washington Cog Railway, opened in two stages during 1868 and 1869, was the first cog tourist railway in the world. Reaching grades of up to 20 percent in places, the train is stopped from running away by the use of a center cog track. *Corbis*

LEFT: The classic photograph taken of the meeting between the Union Pacific and Central Pacific at Promontory Point, Utah, on May 10, 1869. The two locomotives illustrated are, on the left, CP's *Jupiter* and, on the right, UP's No. 119. *Ian Allan Library*

RIGHT: Replica of the Central Pacific's *Jupiter* constructed to mark the centennial of the Golden Spike ceremony. *P. J. Howard*

BELOW: This 4-4-0, No. 173, was the first locomotive to be built completely at the Central Pacific Railroad's workshops at Sacramento, in 1872. *Ian Allan Library*

RIGHT: Built by Smith & Porter in Pittsburgh, *Minnetonka* was the first locomotive purchased by the Northern Pacific Railway, on July 1, 1870, and was used on the construction of the line. *NPR via Ian Allan Library*

BELOW RIGHT: Many early electrification schemes were designed to eliminate smoke pollution. In the early 1890s the B&O constructed a 3.75-mile long electrified connection in Baltimore. The route included the 1.5-mile long Howard Street Tunnel. Electric locomotive No. 1 was built in 1895 to haul steam trains up the tunnel gradient to avoid exhaust problems. *Ian Allan Library*

Chinese laborers at work with pick, shovels, wheelbarrows, and one-horse carts on the long trestle originally built in 1865 on the present Southern Pacific Railroad lines at Sacramento. The picture was taken in 1877 and shows the crude construction methods in use when the first railroad was built across the Sierra Nevada range.
Bettmann/Corbis

FAR LEFT: When this view of the signal tower at the junction of Lake and Wells streets on the New York Elevated Electric was taken in 1919, the junction was the busiest on any railroad in the world. Originally constructed in 1897 the tower was to survive until 1969.
Ian Allan Library

LEFT: The New York, New Haven & Hartford Railroad was a pioneer in the use of 11kV 25-cycle electrification in 1907. This view shows the early days of the electrification with two of the new electric locomotives, headed by No. 029, on a westbound train. Note the unusual triangular overhead.
Ian Allan Library

ABOVE LEFT: In the early years of the twentieth century the Pennsylvania Railroad announced its intention to extend its line into New York and construct a new station on the west side of Manhattan. This scene shows construction of the new station, which took place between 1905 and 1910. *Corbis*

ABOVE: A view of the completed Penn Station taken from the northeast around 1911. The sheer size of the structure in comparison with its surrounds is striking. The station, amidst much controversy, was demolished above platform level in the early 1960s when it was replaced by Madison Square Gardens.

LEFT: Photographed during the first decade of the twentieth century, this shows the railroad station in the Catskills, New York, on the Kaaterskill Railway, which ran during the summer only to take vacationers to resort hotels. *Bettmann/Corbis*

RIGHT: In 1925 the Jersey Central Railroad took delivery of its No. 1000—the first diesel-electric locomotive owned by an American railroad. The locomotive was a joint venture between Alco, General Electric, and Ingersoll-Rand. The locomotive was preserved after retirement in 1957. *GEC*

TOP: Located in Nicholson, Pennsylvania, the Tunkhannock Viaduct (shown during its days as part of Erie-Lackawanna Railroad) was constructed by Delaware, Lackawanna & Western between 1912 and 1915 as part of a cutoff route between Scranton, Pennsylvania, and Hallstead, New Jersey. The 2,375-foot viaduct was then the world's largest concrete bridge. *Ian Allan Library*

ABOVE: The clerestory rolling stock on this Pennsylvania Railroad train pictured at Narberth, Pennsylvania, is typical of the heavyweight coaches used by U.S. railroads during the interwar years. *Ian Allan Library*

RIGHT: Hell Gate Bridge is one of the true engineering marvels in the U.S. Built in 1917, it allows trains from New Haven and Boston to connect with the former Pennsylvania Railroad and thus provide through service south of New York to Philadelphia, Baltimore, and Washington. Here an electric-hauled Amtrak train from Boston moves onto the bridge. *Brian J. Cudahy*

One of two bridges built to span the Mississippi River that were named after Huey P. Long, the governor of the state of Louisiana who was assassinated in September 1935: This bridge was opened in December 1935 and, at 4.5 miles in length, is the longest combined road/rail bridge in the U.S. There are currently plans for the bridge to be expanded. *Southern Pacific*

LEFT: The narrow gauge Georgetown Loop Railroad, part of the Colorado Central Railroad (later Colorado & Southern), was one of Colorado's first tourist attractions when it opened in 1884. This view, showing No. 70 operating over the line at the high bridge, was taken in 1938 shortly before the line's closure. Almost 40 years later, work started to reopen a four-mile section, including reconstruction of the high bridge. The project was completed and the line reopened in 1984.
R. H. Kindig

In 1927 an exhibition and pageant was held to mark the centennial of the meeting that inaugurated the Baltimore & Ohio. In addition to B&O locomotives and rolling stock, equipment from other railroads also operated. Here New York Central Hudson 4-6-4 No. 5205 passes the grandstand; a long line of additional exhibits can be seen in the background. *Ian Allan Library*

New York, New Haven & Hartford Railroad Brill gas-electrics are pictured shortly after delivery in 1937. *Ian Allan Library*

The Zephyr *Burlington's New Motor Train*

DIESEL POWERED
ELECTRICALLY CONTROLLED

A GLEAMING SHAFT OF STAINLESS STEEL

9900

BURLINGTON

UNITED STATES MAIL
RAILWAY POST OFFICE

ABOVE: In 1934 CB&Q launched the *Burlington Zephyr*—a diesel-powered three-coach articulated set that provided seating accommodation for 72 passengers as well as space for baggage and mail. This is the brochure produced by the railway to launch the service. *Ian Allan Library*

LEFT: The passenger accommodations on the *Burlington Zephyr* were largely in the last of the three coaches—illustrated here. The end section of the train allowed twelve passengers to sit in the observation car "parlor." *Ian Allan Library*

The 1930s witnessed a boom in streamlining of both locomotives and rolling stock. Here the streamlined and air-conditioned B&O *Royal Blue* express is photographed en route between Washington and New York crossing the Thomas Viaduct at Relay, Maryland, in the late 1930s. The bridge, originally known as Latrobe's Folly, was constructed between 1833 and 1835. *Ian Allan Library*

LEFT: One of Santa Fe's brand-new 5,400-horsepower A-B-B-A sets of EMD FT locomotives heads over the grades at Cajon Pass, California, with its first eastbound train. *Ian Allan Library*

BELOW LEFT: Taken in 1936, this view shows the pioneer diesel-electric locomotive operated by the B&O. The success of this locomotive encouraged further dieselization on U.S. railroads, ultimately spelling the end of mainline steam. *Ian Allan Library*

RIGHT: In 1937 Santa Fe launched its diesel-powered *Super Chief* service. For the 202 miles between La Junta, Colorado, and Dodge City, Kansas, only 130 minutes were scheduled; with an average speed of 87.2 mph; this was, at the time, the fastest railroad service in the world. *Ian Allan Library*

BELOW RIGHT: One of B&O's new diesel locomotive pairs is pictured on the Washington-Chicago *Capitol Limited*. *Ian Allan Library*

One of the new 3600 H. P. Diesel-Electrics

Exhibit of the
Baltimore & Ohio Railroad

16th Annual Meeting of Mechanical Division
Operations and Maintenance Department
Association of American Railroads

Atlantic City, New Jersey • June 16-23, 1937

The "George H. Emerson"

LEFT: In 1937 Baltimore & Ohio celebrated its 110th anniversary by exhibiting two of its brand-new locomotive classes at Atlantic City, New Jersey. This commemorative brochure (with detail blow-up) was produced in connection with the exhibition. *Ian Allan Library*

FAR LEFT: In July 1946 a double-headed Erie Railroad freight is pictured on the Gulf Summit grade in New York State. *W. R. Osborne*

LEFT: Santa Fe Railway No. 3460, a Hudson 4-6-4, was built by the Baldwin Locomotive Works in 1938. This streamlined locomotive was designed to work prestigious passenger services, such as the *Chief* between Chicago and La Junta, Colorado. *Santa Fe Railway via Ian Allan Library*

RIGHT: "A Speedy Termination of the War." A wartime poster designed by Ernest Hamlin Baker exhorts railroad workers to do their part to help defeat the Germans and Japanese in World War II. *Swim Ink 2, LLC/Corbis*

LEFT: A westbound diesel heading for Long Island City, leaves Jamaica station on August 29, 1956. In the background a New York-bound multiple-unit. *William D. Middleton*

BELOW: Illinois Central introduced this stylish diesel railcar in early 1941. *Ian Allan Library*

A SPEEDY TERMINATION OF THE WAR

This depends more than anything else on the support the United States gives the Allies. Our country cannot do justice to the job, unless railroad men get busy and do their part.... Are you awake to your responsibility?

THE NATION IS COUNTING ON YOU

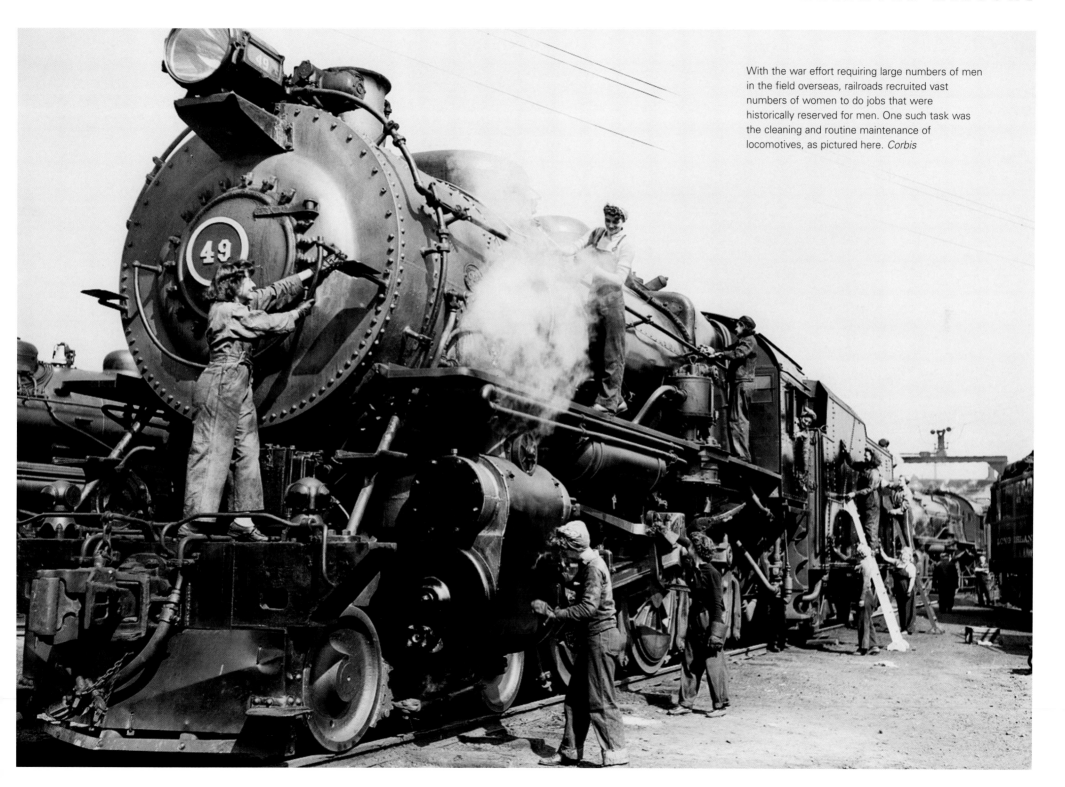

With the war effort requiring large numbers of men in the field overseas, railroads recruited vast numbers of women to do jobs that were historically reserved for men. One such task was the cleaning and routine maintenance of locomotives, as pictured here. *Corbis*

ABOVE: A postcard produced around 1941 for the *Florida Sunbeam*, which connected New York with the Sunshine State. Running southward, the train first traversed the New York Central, switched to Southern Railway trackage, and then finished its journey on the Seaboard Air Line. *Lake Country Museum/Corbis*

RIGHT: A typical scene during the great age of steam. By the late 1940s, with dieselization progressing rapidly, mainline steam was in rapid decline throughout the U.S. and it would not be long before steam-powered trains, outside museums, were consigned to history. *Ian Allan Library*

ABOVE: The opulence of early twentieth-century rolling stock is shown in this view of the interior of the Martha Washington dining car. *Ian Allan Library*

BELOW: Budd announced its RDC in 1949. This example was operated by the Pennsy. *W. A. Burk*

ABOVE RIGHT: Described as a "modern interior" at the time, this was the scene inside a New York Central coach in 1946. *New York Central System via Ian Allan Library*

BELOW: In February 1956 a New York subway train from Times Square to Flushing approaches Queensboro Plaza station, Long Island City. The Queensboro Bridge can be seen in the distance. *B. A. Butt*

RIGHT: The interior of one of the then new Vista-Dome coaches built for the CB&Q. (See also page 51.) *Ian Allan Library*

ABOVE: Classic Northern Pacific poster of Rainier National Park by Gustav Krollmann. *Swim Ink 2, LLC/Corbis*

RIGHT: B&O Pacific No. 6502 was constructed for use on the *Cincinnatian* luxury train from Baltimore to Cincinnati, which was launched in January 1947. *B&O via Ian Allan Library*

FAR RIGHT: In 1949 CB&Q introduced the first Vista-Dome coaches for use on its various *Zephyr* services. The dramatic scenery evident in this photograph shows why the cars were so popular. *CB&Q via Ian Allan Library*

At 8.15 A.M. on April 2, 1956, at Tucson, Arizona, the eastbound *Sunset Limited*, traveling overnight from Los Angeles and hauled by SP No. 6002, gets a cleaning while being refueled. The train is bound for New Orleans. *B. A. Butt*

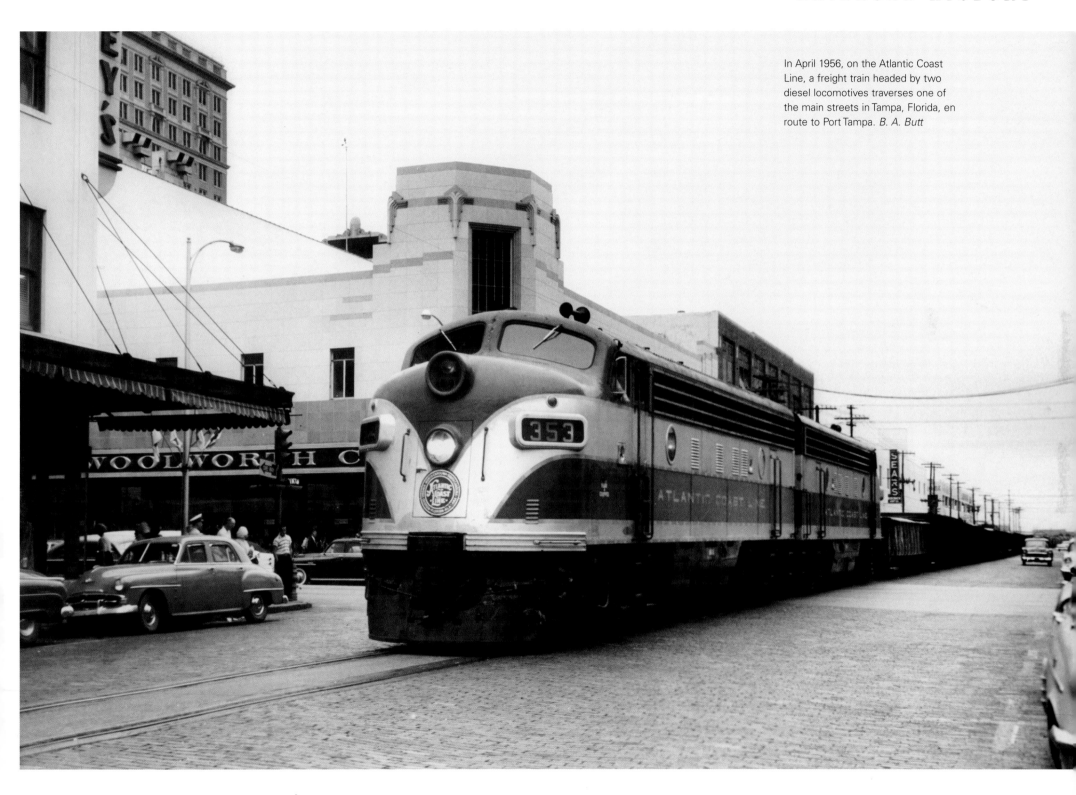

In April 1956, on the Atlantic Coast Line, a freight train headed by two diesel locomotives traverses one of the main streets in Tampa, Florida, en route to Port Tampa. *B. A. Butt*

RIGHT: Amtrak GE P42-9DC locomotives Nos. AMTK145 and AMTK144 pass Helendale between Victorville and Barstow, deadheading the American Orient Express passenger set from from Los Angeles to Albuquerque on August 24, 2005. *Colin J. Marsden*

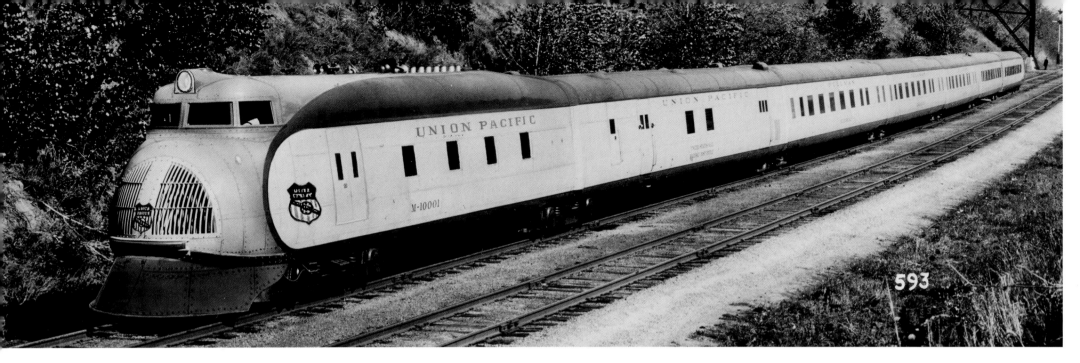

TOP: Union Pacific's *City of Portland*, one of a number of streamlined passenger trains introduced by the UP. The first of these was launched in February 1934 marking the start of the streamlined era on U.S. railroads. *Ian Allan Library*

ABOVE: On April 17, 1958, a westbound freight approaches Banning, California, from Indio on the Southern Pacific main line into Los Angeles from southern Arizona. *B. A. Butt*

RIGHT: In the years after the end of World War II, mainline steam rapidly disappeared from U.S. railroads; these two Reading Railroad locomotives are recorded toward the end of their working life. *Harry Luff Collection/Online Transport Archive*

LEFT: In May 1968 Burlington E8 No. 9940 departs from Chicago Union Station with an evening commuter train. *R. K. Evans*

ABOVE: Increasingly common after the mid-1950s, hood units, like that on the right, began to replace streamliners, especially in freight service. Still at work in May 1968 was Illinois Central's passenger locomotive No. 4019, seen alongside GP9 No. 9208. *R. K. Evans*

LEFT: The desolate Union Station at Kansas City, Missouri, was once one of the busiest in the country. Here, shortly before the takeover of long-distance passenger service by Amtrak, Santa Fe's *Texas Chief* departs from the station. The lack of passenger services in the station demonstrates the sharp decline of the American passenger train after 1960. *Brian J. Cuddahy*

By the early 1970s Alco PA diesel locomotives were disappearing. In 1974, only four were still in service—all on the Delaware & Hudson and pictured here on a special train in November of that year. Originally built in 1947 for Santa Fe, this quartet was sold to Mexico in 1978. *Bruce Russell*

ABOVE: An Amtrak Turboliner from Chicago is pictured on arrival in Milwaukee. *C. R. Davis*

LEFT: These 1928-built 3,000V dc electric multiple units, in service with the South Shore Railway in Chicago, were almost fifty years old when recorded in 1975. *Bruce Russell*

ABOVE RIGHT: The LRC (Light Rapid Comfortable), pictured on a demonstration run in Boston, was tested by Amtrak in the 1980s, but never purchased by the American passenger carrier. Canada's VIA Rail was the only customer for the LRC. *Amtrak*

FAR RIGHT: A Budd SP2000 diesel railcar delivered in 1980 for service in Connecticut. *Ian Allan Library*

RIGHT: An array of superpower on June 11, 1979, leads Amtrak's *Coast Starlight*, pictured at San José. The four locomotives provide the train with a total of some 12,000 horsepower. *John A. M. Vaughan*

OPPOSITE, ABOVE: On June 3, 1979, an 11,000-ton coal train heads into the Mojave Desert in California headed by three Santa Fe GP40X diesel locomotives. An additional three locomotives, radio controlled, are located in the middle of the train as helper units. *Andrew Taylor*

OPPOSITE, BELOW: In the mid-1970s Amtrak acquired seven Rohr-built five-car Turboliner trains based on French technology. One of the sets is pictured emerging from the south portal of Cold Spring Tunnel alongside the Hudson River with an New York-Niagara Falls *Empire State Express*. *Amtrak*

LEFT: A westbound freight from Salt Lake City, Utah, to Stockton, California, passes under California Highway 70 near Pulga, in the Feather River Canyon, on the Western Pacific Railroad. *Andrew Taylor*

PAGE 70: Headed by a trio of specially maintained 1955-built EMD F9 locomotives, the Denver & Rio Grande Western Railroad's *Rio Grande Zephyr* pauses at Grand Junction, Colorado, on its run from Salt Lake City to Denver on June 2, 1980. *Andrew Taylor*

PAGE 71: Four units head a freight from Cowan, Tennessee, on the Louisville & Nashville Railroad. The train will be assisted by helper locomotives, positioned at the rear of the train, for the climb up the grade to Cumberland Tunnel. *R. S. Greenwood*

BELOW: The Los Angeles-Seattle Coast *Starlight* pauses at Portland, Oregon, on June 9, 1980. *Andrew Taylor*

RIGHT: A Rio Grande SD45 leads a set of five locomotives powering a freight train through Glenwood Springs, Colorado. *P. J. Howard*

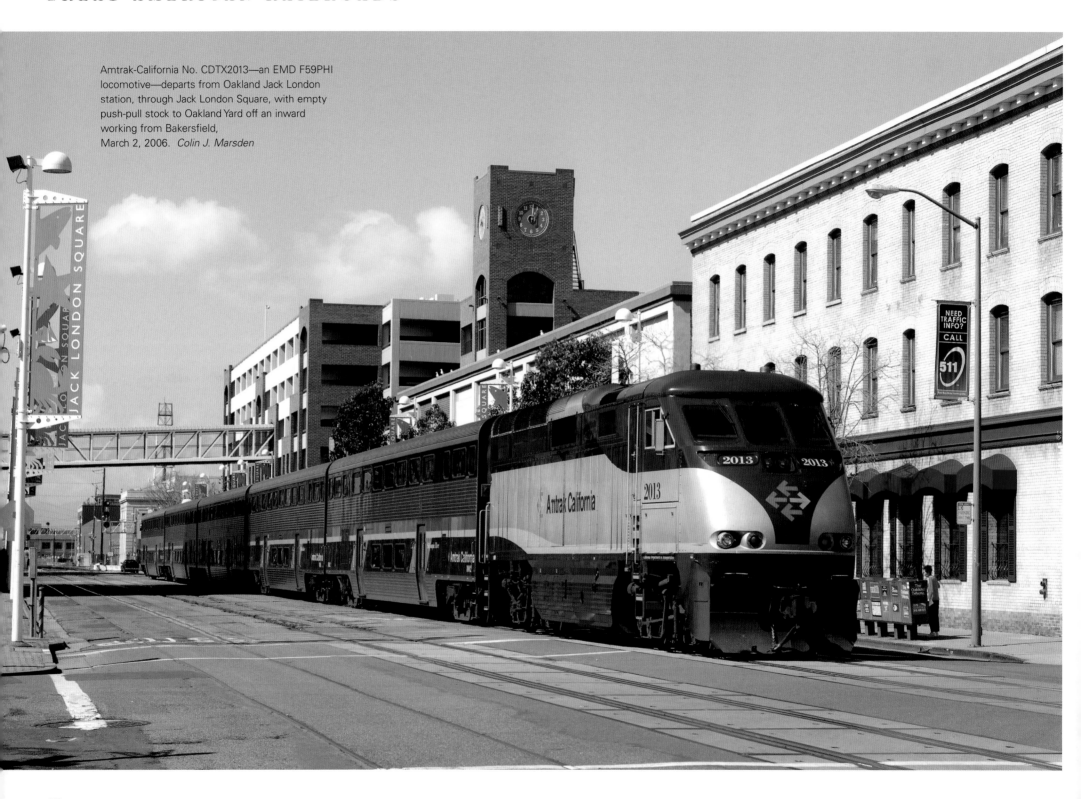

Amtrak-California No. CDTX2013—an EMD F59PHI locomotive—departs from Oakland Jack London station, through Jack London Square, with empty push-pull stock to Oakland Yard off an inward working from Bakersfield, March 2, 2006. *Colin J. Marsden*

Today's locos cannot compare to the sleek beauty of the immediate postwar classes.
Time Life Pictures/Getty Images

Railroad Companies

The history of American railroading is dominated by the great companies; over the years many of these companies have taken over other operators or been subsumed into great conglomerates. Unlike Europe and many other parts of the world where railways have become in whole or in part state controlled, the railroad industry in the USA has been primarily dominated by private enterprise. It was only after many of the major companies withdrew for commercial reasons from the running of long-distance passenger services that a publicly funded organisation, known for short as Amtrak, was established to take over these services and the government also took action over other failing lines (for example the creation of Conrail in 1976). Following mega-mergers the USA is now dominated by the "Big Four" railroad companies: Burlington Northern & Santa Fe; CSX; Norfolk Southern; and Union Pacific.

RIGHT: An early 1960s view sees a Santa Fe diesel locomotive departing from Chicago with a passenger train; at this date long-distance passenger services remained in the hands of the traditional carriers. By the end of the decade, economics decreed that such services were no longer viable and Amtrak soon took over. *Harry Luff Collection/Online Transport Archive*

FAR RIGHT: While mainline services faced competition from air and road, the demise of steam and changes to the economy led to the birth of preservation. The narrow-gauge Cumbres & Toltec Scenic Railroad that travels between New Mexico and Colorado, is an example of tourism taking over from industry. *Aurora/Getty Images*

Amtrak

The National Rail Passenger Corporation, known as Amtrak for short, was established in 1970 to take over long-distance passenger trains from the private railroads. Most of these services, facing stiff competition from the airlines and private automobile travel, had been losing money. Involvement in Amtrak was voluntary but most of the prior long-distance carriers transferred their service. When established, Amtrak operated—but did not own the track—over some 26,000 route miles, although this represented a 40 percent reduction over the mileage operated by the private companies. Even with this reduction, Amtrak never has come close to covering its cost and must be subsidized by the government. This federal support has always been tenuous and over the years the passenger operator has been forced to reduce the number of services that it operates.

RIGHT: Amtrak's *Southwest Limited*—successor to Santa Fe's *Super Chief* and today known as the *Southwest Chief*—reaches the summit tunnel on New Mexico's Raton Pass in mid-1981, during the train's westward trek from Chicago to Los Angeles. *P. J. Howard*

FAR RIGHT: Penn Central No. 6163 hauls a freight east of Horseshoe Curve, Altoona, Pennsylvania. *H. Bongaardt*

OVE: The northbound *Connecticut Yankee* from
shington, D.C., to Springfield, Massachusetts,
ses at Trenton, New Jersey. *Chris Shaw*

RIGHT: Amtrak GE-built Class P42s Nos. AMTK182 and
AMTK122 pass Pinole with train No. 11, the 10:00 Seattle–Los
Angeles "Coast Starlight," March 3. 2006. *Colin J. Marsden*

Atchison, Topeka & Santa Fe Railway

Better known as the Santa Fe, construction of the AT&SF started at Topeka, Kansas, in 1872 and the trackage reached Los Angeles by 1887. Later extensions saw the company reach north to Oakland, on San Francisco Bay, and south to Galveston, Texas. In addition to its speedy cross-country mainline, the Santa Fe built up an impressive network of branch lines, especially in Kansas, Oklahoma, and Texas. By 1931 the Santa Fe reached its peak, with more than 13,500 route miles—for many years, it was the longest railroad in the U.S. The Santa Fe was predominantly a freight hauler, but it also boasted an impressive lineup of top-notch passenger trains in the pre-Amtrak years. The company used steam until 1959 but was a pioneer in the use of diesel power, acquiring its first locomotives in 1935. Santa Fe's striking "Warbonnet" paint scheme remains the most popular diesel livery in U.S. railroading history. In the mid-1980s, Santa Fe attempted to merge with its long-time rival, Southern Pacific, but was denied by the Interstate Commerce Commission. The company eventually merged with Burlington Northern in 1995 to become BNSF.

LEFT: The engineer, doing a little maintenance on a Santa Fe 5001-class locomotive, is dwarfed by the 2-10-4's 6-foot, 2-inch driving wheels and cylinders. The locomotive weighed a total of 272 tons, and the tender an additional 180 tons. *Ian Allan Library*

BELOW: A line-up of Santa Fe streamlined trains at Chicago. These are, from the left: the *Super Chief*— all-standard sleeping car train; *El Capitan*—all-coach train; the *Chief*—daily standard sleeping car train; a second *Super Chief*; and, a second *El Capitan*. The *Super Chief* and *El Capitan* operated twice weekly between Chicago and Los Angeles on a 40-hour schedule in each direction and the *Chief* operated between the same points on a 48-hour schedule. *Santa Fe Railway via Ian Allan Library*

RIGHT: October 6, 2004, 12:18—Nos. SF2619, SF2595, and SF2463 await a line up at Jim Grey, on the line between Mojave and Barstow. The train is from Borax and is bound for Barstow yard. Today it is only such local freights that produce true Santa Fe traction consists.
Colin J. Marsden

Boston & Maine

The B&M was the largest railroad operator in New England and represented the merger of some 100 smaller companies, the earliest of which—the Andover & Wilmington— was opened in 1836 linking the states of Massachusetts and Maine. At its peak, in the early 1920s, the B&M extended over 2,248 route miles. The company constructed, with work being completed in 1876, the 4.75-mile long Hoosac Tunnel between Greenfield and upstate New York; this was the longest tunnel in the U.S. when constructed and remains in use today. When the B&M was predominantly steam-operated, locomotives were piloted through the tunnel by electric locomotives to avoid smoke polluting the tunnel. Although some commuter services still operate into B&M's Boston North station, the remainder of the modern-day traffic is freight only. B&M became part of the Guilford Rail System in 1983, joining former competitor Maine Central.

RIGHT: B&M 2-8-0 No. 2394 was a K6 class dating from 1935. The locomotive is pictured leading a local passenger train. *Ivan W. Saunders*

FAR RIGHT: A B&M commuter train leaves Boston for a run to South Acton in early 1976. Suburban services were, by this date, the only passenger services operated by the B&M and were subsidized by the Massachusetts Bay Transportation Authority. Inset image shows logo color. *Brian J. Cuddahy; Time Life Pictures/Getty Images*

Baltimore & Ohio Railroad

Accepted as the first railroad in the U.S. to build a line for general traffic, construction of the B&O commenced in July 4, 1828, and the first 13 miles from Baltimore to Ellicott Mills opened—using horses for power—in May 1830. On August 1830 steam first appeared and over the following years the line was gradually extended, reaching Cumberland, 178 miles from Baltimore, in 1842. The next section, through the Allegheny Mountains, took eleven years to complete but the line opened through to Wheeling, West Virginia, on January 1, 1853. During the 1860s, the B&O suffered significant damage as a result of the Civil War but, with peace restored in 1865, expansion continued. The B&O retained its independence until the 1970s when it became part of the Chessie System, and later CSX Transportation.

ABOVE: Passenger accommodation on the early B&O was relatively primitive and owed much to the contemporary stagecoach—as this reconstruction emphasizes. *Ian Allan Library*

RIGHT: Headed by No. 5227, B&O's *Capitol Limited* is captured on film in the picturesque Potomac River valley en route from New York to Chicago. The *Capitol Limited* was one of the first trains in the world to be air-conditioned throughout. Inset, B&O box car logo. *Ian Allan Library; Time Life Pictures/Getty Images*

Burlington Northern

The railroad was established in 1970 by the merger of four earlier companies: Chicago, Burlington & Quincy; Northern Pacific; Great Northern; and Spokane, Portland & Seattle. It merged with the Santa Fe in 1995 to become part of the new BNSF.

LEFT: Crowds wait to board two Budd-built RDCs at Cleveland in 1961; the RDCs, introduced by Budd in 1949, were designed to reduce the cost of operating passenger services and could operate singly or in multiple. *Harry Luff Collection/Online Transport Archive*

RIGHT: Burlington Northern's streamlined E8s, such as the 9906, spent their last years in service hauling Metra commuter trains from downtown Chicago to the city's western suburbs. *Ian Allan Library*

Burlington Northern Santa Fe

The Burlington Northern Santa Fe (BNSF) was formed in 1995 by the merger between the Burlington Northern and the Santa Fe railroads.

Chesapeake & Ohio

Based in Cleveland, Ohio, Chessie System formed with the 1973 merger of the Baltimore & Ohio, Chesapeake & Ohio, Pere Marquette, and Western Maryland railroads. It was known for its brightly colored locomotives and for its steam specials that delighted history-minded railroad buffs. Chessie later merged with the Seaboard System to become CSX.

Chicago, Burlington & Quincy

Serving America's flat agricultural heartland, the Burlington—as the company was known—was relatively easy to construct except for major river crossings, including multiple bridges over the Mississippi and Missouri, and a single bridge over the Ohio to reach Paducah, Kentucky. Burlington's silver, streamlined Zephyrs are an important part of American passenger train lore. The Burlington became part of Burlington Northern in 1970 and part of the BNSF in 1995.

LEFT: Doublestack container trains significantly improved the economics of long-haul intermodal freight trains and allowed BNSF to become a major link in moving goods manufactured in Asia, hauled across the Pacific on ships, and handed off to railroads on the West Coast. *Colin J. Marsden*

BELOW: CB&Q No. 4960 traveled 100 miles in exactly 100 minutes—averaging 60 mph—a considerable achievement for a steam locomotive or, as the photographer commented: "They said it couldn't be done—but she did it!" *Thomas T. Taber*

RIGHT: The BNSF has its headquarters in Fort Worth, Texas, and is not only one of the largest railroad networks in North America but also one of the top transporters of intermodal traffic. It moves more grain than any other American railroad and hauls enough coal to generate a tenth of the electricity produced in the United States.
Colin J. Marsden

ABOVE: CB&Q was one of three partners in the *California Zephyr* along with Denver & Rio Grande and Western Pacific. Here the train is pictured proceeding along Third Avenue in Oakland, California, hauled by three EMD diesel locomotives. *Ian Allan Library*

RIGHT: CB&Q was one of the few railroads to buy EMD SD24 diesel locomotives. The "SD" stood for "Special Duty" and for Burlington the "SD" concerned was high-speed freight. Sixteen of the diesel units were acquired from General Motors in May and June 1959. *Ian Allan Library*

RIGHT: Soo Line box car logo. The Soo took over the Milwaukee Road in 1980 (see also page 122). *Time Life Pictures/Getty Images*

BELOW: Chicago, Milwaukee, St. Paul & Pacific Railroad electric locomotive No. 10252. *Ian Allan Library*

BELOW RIGHT: C&NW No. 10035 was the largest storage battery electric locomotive in the world. *R. A. Learmouth*

Chicago, Milwaukee, St. Paul & Pacific

The first section of the future CMStP&P—better known as the Milwaukee Road—opened in 1851 as the Milwaukee & Waukesha Railroad and the line reached Chicago in 1873. Roughly 6,000 route miles were in operation by 1900, with the company's routes extending as far as Kansas. The company reached the Pacific Ocean in 1909 and changed its name accordingly in 1913. The Milwaukee struggled in the 1960s and 1970s, facing stiff competition operating in regions (upper Midwest and Pacific Northwest) with too many main lines and not enough freight. Things deteriorated even more after a proposed merger with Chicago & North Western was rejected and several of its key competitors merged to form Burlington Northern. The company went bankrupt in December 1977, abandoned the Pacific extension in 1980, and reorganized as a smaller regional company. Despite the restructuring, the Milwaukee continued to struggle and was taken over by Soo Line in February 1985. Soo Line, in turn, was taken over in 1990 by Canadian Pacific.

Chicago & North Western

Galena & Chicago Union Railroad, a predecessor of the C&NW, was the first railroad to operate west of Chicago when it opened in October 1848. C&NW itself was established in 1859 and by 1900 operated over some 8,300 miles of track. Despite being an underdog in a region crisscrossed with too much track and several powerful rail companies, C&NW survived, primarily by serving agricultural customers. The company expanded in the 1960s by acquiring Minneapolis & St. Louis and Chicago Great Western, ultimately increasing its network to nearly 10,000 route miles. In the 1970s and 1980s C&NW grew even stronger, by purchasing profitable parts of the failed Rock Island, becoming a major player in the booming Wyoming coalfields, forming a strategic alliance with Union Pacific, and dumping many of the farm-country branches on which it previously relied. C&NW remained independent until 1988 when it became part of the Union Pacific.

Conrail

Established as a government-owned corporation in 1976, Conrail—short for Consolidated Rail Corporation—represented a merger of Penn Central, Erie-Lackawanna, Central of New Jersey, Lehigh & Hudson River, Lehigh & New England, Lehigh Valley, and Reading railroads. Conrail eventually became a highly profitable venture and returned to private ownership. Following a heated takeover battle, Conrail was split between CSX Transportation and Norfolk Southern.

Delaware & Hudson

The first U.S. railroad to operate steam locomotives regularly, the Delaware & Hudson survived for more than 150 years before becoming part of Guilford System in 1984. Guilford sold the company in 1988 and in 1990 it became a subsidiary of Canadian Pacific.

RIGHT: Conrail No. 6575 heads an eastbound freight on the Berkshire Division at Hinsdale, Massachusetts, on July 7, 1989. *Thomas Hildreth*

FAR RIGHT: Delaware & Hudson 4-6-6-4 No. 1500 is pictured hauling a freight. *Ian Allan Library*

Denver & Rio Grande

Facing the challenge of Colorado's Rocky Mountains ex-Confederate General William Jackson Palmer adopted the 3-foot, 0 inch gauge for construction of his railroad line south from Denver. Work on the Denver & Rio Grande started in 1871 and by 1872 the track had reached Pueblo, where Palmer established the Central Colorado Improvement Company, a company that later was to provide the bulk of the line's traffic until the mid-1950s. In 1873 financial troubles led to delays and in the process the most obvious route to the south—Raton Pass—was lost to the Santa Fe. Palmer then decided to head west, reaching Alamosa via the Sangre de Cristo Range and Veta Pass, in 1878 but again the line's path was blocked by another company's line. In 1879 the courts ruled in favor of the Rio Grande but the railroad collapsed financially and the line came under the influence of Jay Gould, who also controlled the Union Pacific. Under Gould's guidance a settlement was reached which allowed the Rio Grande to expand further. However, as the line expanded, Gould's influence declined and Palmer regained control. In the 1880s, Palmer decided to convert the principal Rio Grande routes to standard gauge, resulting in the gradual decline of the remaining narrow gauge lines. As a standard-gauge railway the Rio Grande continued to grow, but eventually went bankrupt. In 1921 the company emerged from bankruptcy as the Denver & Rio Grande Western; it merged with the Denver & Salt Lake in 1947 and, in 1988, the line was merged with the Southern Pacific at which time the D&RGW name was dropped. The enlarged Southern Pacific merged with Union Pacific in 1996.

LEFT: Denver & Rio Grande Western No. 1604 was a 4-8-2, typical of the locomotives used by the railroad after the bulk of its lines had been converted to standard gauge. *Ian Allan Library*

ABOVE: Merger partners alongside each other: locomotives from South Pacific and Denver & Rio Grande Western pose together in 1988. *Southern Pacific*

LEFT: K36 class No. 483, built by Baldwin in 1925, is pictured about to depart Salida for Monarch, leading a train of empty gondolas on the narrow gauge Denver & Rio Grande. *Ian Allan Library*

RIGHT: Great Northern box car logo. *Time Life Pictures/Getty Images*

BELOW: Two GN Z1-class electric locomotives haul a passenger train. The class was introduced in the 1920s when the electrification of the route was upgraded to 11.5kV. *Ian Allan Library*

Great Northern

Driven by the ambition of one man, James J. Hill, the GN was constructed to the north of the Northern Pacific. The line to the Pacific Northwest was completed on September 18, 1893, and included the 7.75-mile long Cascade Tunnel, which became the longest tunnel on a U.S. railroad. The line through Cascade Tunnel was electrified in 1909 and replaced by 11.5kV in 1927. A longer Cascade Tunnel was opened two years later. The electrified section was ultimately converted to diesel power. The GN became part of the Burlington Northern in 1970, which, in turn, became BNSF in 1995.

Illinois Central

When it received its charter on February 10, 1851, the Illinois Central was the longest railroad then promoted in the U.S. It was also the first to receive land grants as a subsidy on completion. The 705-mile-long line opened in September 1856. Built originally to 5-foot, 0-inch gauge, the line was eventually converted to standard gauge. The company expanded by taking over a number of other railroads, reaching as far as Kansas City in the west and Indianapolis in the east. In 1972 it merged with Gulf, Mobile & Ohio to form the Illinois Central Gulf. The company sold much of the ex-GMO trackage in 1985 before itself becoming a subsidiary of Canadian National in 1999.

LEFT: Metra commuter trains—such as this IC-operated job with a string of double-deck coaches—follow Illinois Central trackage south out of downtown Chicago. *Ian Allan Library*

Long Island

Receiving its charter in 1834, the Long Island Rail Road provided the original line between New York and Boston. The company was acquired by the Pennsylvania Railroad in 1900 and electrified as a commuter route serving the Pennsy's new Central station in New York. Financial problems led to the line going bankrupt in 1949. It continued to operate, in an increasingly dilapidated way, until 1964 when it was acquired by the New York State Metropolitan Transit Authority under whose aegis the line was modernized.

Maine Central

A relatively small railroad, the Maine Central was famous for running all-Pullman services, such as the *Bay Harbor Express*, conveying the rich and famous from the major cities to their vacation retreats. Maine Central became part of Guilford System in 1981; New England's other major carrier, Boston & Maine, joined the new railroad two years later.

RIGHT: GP38 locomotives 262, 57, and 52 haul a Guilford System freight out of Bangor, Maine, heading for Pentland, Maine, on July 25, 1985. Even for years after the end of the independent MEC, all three locomotives remain adorned in the Maine Central green-and-yellow livery. *Peter J. Howard*

New York, New Haven & Hartford

The New Haven's earliest predecessor was the Granite Railway of Boston, which dated to 1826 and building the Bunker Hill monument. The New Haven itself was the result of an amalgamation of some 200 other companies. Among trains operated was the *Merchants Limited*, the last all-parlor train in the U.S. The railroad merged with the Pennsylvania and New York Central in 1967 to form Penn Central, and later became part of Conrail in 1976.

RIGHT: New Haven box car logo. *Time Life Pictures/Getty Images*

BELOW: New York Central's streamlined *Mercury* pictured at its launch in 1936 with a string of heavyweight coaches specially rebuilt for the new service. The locomotive, rated at 4,075hp, was expected to be able to haul express trains at up to 90 mph. *Ian Allan Library*

New York Central

The oldest section of the future New York Central was the Mohawk & Hudson Railroad between Albany and Schenectady, which was incorporated in 1826 and opened five years later. The name New York Central first appeared in 1853. Among lines that were ultimately to form part of the company were the New York Central & Hudson River and the Lake Shore & Michigan railroads. One of the line's most famous locomotives, No. 999, built for the Chicago fair of 1893, achieved a speed of 112 mph over a measured mile—a record that was to survive for many years The New York Central merged with the Pennsylvania Railroad in 1968 to become Penn Central. It was then subsumed into Conrail in 1976.

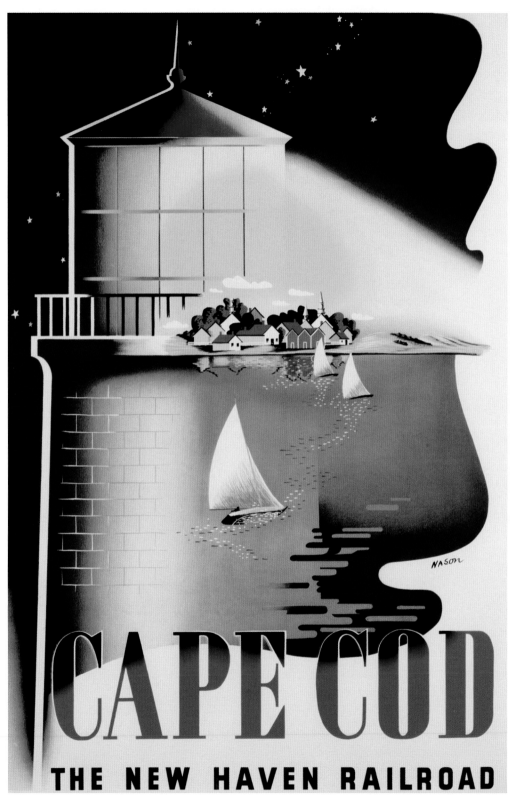

PAGE 112: From a promotional flyer produced in 1934 to mark the launch of the New York Central's streamlined trains; the first locomotive in the class was named *Commodore Vanderbilt* after the founder of the railroad. *Ian Allan Library*

PAGE 113: In February 1956 two NYC Alco-built switchers are pictured at Weehawken terminal with a passenger train awaiting early homeward-bound commuters. The Empire State Building can be seen in the distance. *B. A. Butt*

Norfolk & Western

Norfolk & Western had its origins in the City Point Rail Road, which opened out of Petersburg, Virginia, on September 7, 1838. Other earlier constituents included the Norfolk & Petersburg Railway, the Southside Railroad, and the Virginia & Tennessee Railroad. The company became known as the Atlantic, Mississippi & Ohio Railroad, before becoming the Norfolk & Western in 1881. Unlike other U.S. railroads, the N&W persisted with steam power until a very late date, in part because as the nation's premier coal-hauler, it had access to a ready, cheap supply of fuel for its steamers. N&W purchased the last new steam locomotive constructed for use on a U.S. railroad, No. 244, which entered service in 1953. But the N&W could not hold out against the trend and on April 4, 1960, it ran its last steam-hauled service. In the mid-1950s the N&W extended over some 2,100 route miles; over the next twenty years it expanded rapidly by acquiring other railroads, reaching 7,500 miles of track by 1975. Among companies acquired were the Virginian Railroad in 1959 and the New York, Chicago & St Louis in 1964. In 1982 N&W merged with Southern Railway to form Norfolk Southern; this company acquired a significant part of Conrail in 1999.

ABOVE: One of the premier trains in the U.S. was the New York Central's *Twentieth Century Limited*, which ran overnight between New York and Chicago. Here it is pictured in the late 1950s behind two EMD diesel locomotives. *Brian J. Cuddahy*

RIGHT: N&W GP9 No. 3494 heads a Dearborn-Orland Park commuter train in south Chicago. A number of these hood units—designed for freight hauling—were fitted with steam-heating generators and high-speed trucks for passenger service. *R. K. Evans*

Norfolk Southern

Formed in 199 as a result of the merger between Norfolk & Western and Southern Railway, Norfolk Southern now operates over a network of more than 21,000 route miles.

LEFT: BNSF4079, BNSF4188, BNSF4918, and BNSF5115 pass Bealville, powering a northbound intermodal service, October 1, 2004. *Colin J. Marsden*

ABOVE: One of Northern Pacific's 4-6-6-4 steam locomotives, which were designed for both freight and passenger service. They were 127 feet long and 17 feet high with 5-foot, 9-inch drive wheels. The tender accommodated 27 tons of coal and 22,000 gallons of water. *Northern Pacific via Ian Allan Library*

Northern Pacific

The NP received its charter from President Lincoln in 1864 to construct a line over a route that had been originally surveyed in 1804 by Rogers and Clark. Despite the advantage of an earlier survey, construction was slow and in 1873 financial problems resulted in work being suspended for six years. However, use of the incomplete railroad by troops during the Sioux rising of 1876 demonstrated the importance of the line and that it could be used in harsh climatic conditions. Work restarted in 1879 with the line being completed on 21 April 1883; thus the second transcontinental route was finished. The NP became part of the Burlington Northern in 1970 and of BNSF in 1995.

ABOVE: Northern Pacific Railroad's *North Coast Limited* is shown awaiting departure from Seattle in October 1957. *J. N. Westwood*

RIGHT: "Alaska"—a poster designed by Sidney Laurence promoting the Northern Pacific Railway. *Swim Ink 2, LLC/Corbis*

Penn Central

Penn Central was formed in 1968 as a result of the merger between New York Central, Pennsylvania and New York, New Haven & Hartford railroads. Penn Central suffered severe financial problems from the start, but was rescued by the government, along with other struggling Eastern carriers, with the formation of Conrail in 1976.

BELOW: Penn Central No. 4304 hauls the *Juniata* as its passes the Rockville signal tower, near Harrisburg, Pennsylvania, on October 9, 1969. *H. Bongaardt*

Pennsylvania

The origins of the Pennsylvania Railroad date back to November 12, 1831, and the opening of the Camden & Amboy Railroad in New Jersey. Steam provided power from the outset. The line's first engine was named *John Bull*; appropriately the locomotive had been built in England and shipped across the Atlantic. The "Pennsy," as the company was nicknamed, received its own charter in 1846 for the construction of the line between Pittsburgh and Philadelphia. Serving eight of the country's ten largest cities and with some 10,000 route miles, the Pennsy was by 1874 the largest railroad company in the U.S. An ambitious railroad, the Pennsy eventually constructed one of the greatest stations ever built in the U.S.—Pennsylvania Station in New York—and was among the pioneers of electric traction; it possessed one of the largest electrified networks in the U.S., reflecting its important role as a carrier of commuters into major northeastern cities. The Pennsy became part of Penn Central in 1968 and Conrail in 1976.

LEFT: The classic lines of an ex-Pennsylvania Railroad GG1 in Penn Central livery pictured in Stadium Yard, Philadelphia. *Harry Luff Collection/Online Transport Archive*

ABOVE: One of the classic designs of locomotive operated by the Pennsy was the GG1— an electric class first introduced in 1935 as a joint venture between the railroad and Westinghouse. The last examples of the class were not retired until 1983 and were the last Raymond Loewy-designed railroad equipment to operate. Restored GG1 No. 4877 was one of the trio selected to operate the farewell specials on October 29, 1983. *Alfred Gaus*

Soo Line

Soo Line was originally established as a result of the merger between the Duluth, South Shore & Atlantic, Wisconsin Central, and Minneapolis, St. Paul, & Sault Ste. Marie railroads in 1961. In 1985 Soo Line acquired the downsized Milwaukee Road before the company was acquired by Canadian Pacific in 1990.

Southern Pacific

One of the great names in U.S. railroading, Southern Pacific first appeared in 1865. One of its subsidiary companies—Central Pacific (leased from 1885 and absorbed in 1955)—constructed the first transcontinental route in North America in conjunction with the Union Pacific, the great meeting being marked at Promontory Point, Utah, on May 10, 1869. SP continued to grow rapidly, achieving a maximum network of more than 16,000 route-miles, including more than 1,000 miles of electrified line. Among records claimed by the SP was ownership of the then-longest railroad bridge in the world—some 13 miles in length across the Great Salt Lake (now converted into a causeway)—and the longest combined road/rail bridge in the world—the Huey P. Long bridge at New Orleans. Among notable companies also taken over by SP were the Denver & Rio Grande Western and St. Louis Southwestern (Cotton Belt) railroads. In 1996 SP merged with Union Pacific, with the new company retaining the UP name.

LEFT: A Southern Pacific locomotive, No. 3764, hauls a 100-car train upgrade without helpers in California's Sierra Nevada. *Southern Pacific via Ian Allan Library*

ABOVE: A westbound Southern Pacific freight loops under itself on the famed Tehachapi Loop in California on May 30, 1979. *Andrew Taylor*

LEFT: Departing from Ogden, Utah, this westbound Southern Pacific freight heads across the Salt Lake on the Lucin Cutoff. *P. J. Howard*

ABOVE: "Crossing Great Salt Lake on Southern Pacific" by Haines Hall. *Swim Ink 2, LLC/Corbis*

ABOVE RIGHT: Three box car logos. *Time Life Pictures/Getty Images*

BELOW RIGHT: The *City of Los Angeles* was one of a number of streamlined trains introduced by Union Pacific in the 1930s. *Union Pacific via Ian Allan Library*

Southern Railway

Southern Railway has several claims to fame. One of its predecessors—the South Carolina Railroad—operated the first scheduled railway service in the U.S., on December 25, 1830. It also possessed the steepest grade on any major railway route in the U.S.—nearly 5 percent. In addition, unlike most other railroads that left their locomotives black, SR was unusual in painting its locomotives emerald green. The company became the Southern Railway in 1894 and its main routes linked Washington with New Orleans, Atlanta, and Cincinnati. SR continued to expand during the postwar years, taking over the South Georgia and Cincinnati, New Orleans & Texas Pacific in 1963. It merged with the Norfolk & Western in 1982 to become Norfolk Southern.

Union Pacific

One of the great names in U.S. railroading history, Union Pacific traces its beginnings to the first transcontinental railroad that started its way west from Omaha on June 10, 1865. Four years later, at Promontory Point, Utah, on May 10, 1869, the dream of constructing a railroad across the United States was achieved when the Union Pacific and Central Pacific lines met. While the latter was destined for a relatively short independent existence, Union Pacific has gone from strength to strength to become one of the dominant forces in U.S. railroading. Already incorporating the Western Pacific, Texas & Pacific and Missouri Pacific railroads, the UP expanded further with the 1982 takeover of the Missouri-Kansas-Texas and its 1988 acquisition of Chicago & North Western. In 1996 another merger, this time with Southern Pacific, saw Union Pacific emerge as one of the country's "Big Four" railroad companies, operating over nearly 33,000 route miles.

On July 6, 1955, Union Pacific No. 9000, the original 4-12-2, heads eastbound towards Omaha with a freight train. The locomotive was preserved after retirement. *W. H. N. Rossiter*

A westbound UP freight hauled by a GE U28C and two EMD SD40-2 locomotives is seen at Henefer, Utah, on its way to Ogden on June 19, 1983. *Andrew Taylor*

SD40-2-class UP3227, UP3400, and UP3658 pass through Jack London Square, with a baretable train heading towards San Jose and the south, March 2, 2006. Street running in California is not as profilic as it used to be, but the Jack London area of Oakland sees around 40 trains every day.
Colin J. Marsden

BELOW: Union Pacific 4-12-2 No. 9505 pictured at Great Island, Nebraska. *Ian Allan Library*

RIGHT: UP4620, UP3919, and UP9559 pass Frost, west of Victorville, with a westbound stack train, October 1, 2003. This service was operating from Salt Lake City to Long Beach via Las Vegas. *Colin J. Marsden*

Western Pacific

Toward the end of the nineteenth century George J. Gould had a dream: he wanted to construct another transcontinental railroad. Furthermore, Gould's dream was to have the entire west-east line operated by a single company. He already, courtesy of his father, controlled much of the route but, ultimately his dream was thwarted by his failure to take over an existing line between Salt Lake City and the Pacific. Construction of the Western Pacific—and fulfillment of Gould's dream—was completed in November 1909, but the financial pressures of building the railroad resulted in the family losing control of the railroad. WP ultimately went bankrupt twice in the ensuing years, in 1915 and 1935. In 1949, in conjunction with CB&Q and D&RGW, Western Pacific launched the *California Zephyr*—a 53-hour journey between Oakland and Chicago that offered passengers a superb scenic ride. Until the service ended in 1970, the five sets used on the route provided a daily service unrivalled in terms of facilities offered—including the much-loved Vista-Domes. Western Pacific lost its independence in 1982 when it became part of the Union Pacific.

White Pass & Yukon Railway

The first section of this 3 foot, 0 inch gauge railroad was opened on July 21, 1898, from the port of Skagway to Whitehorse, Yukon Territory, to serve the Klondike gold rush. The line was eventually extended to a total of 571 miles and reached Dawson City. Declining traffic resulted in the line's closure in 1982, but the first twenty miles from Skagway were reopened for tourist traffic in 1988 and, ultimately, a total of 111 miles to Whitehorse are planned for tourist services.

LEFT: On June 8, 1979, a WP Stockton-Salt Lake piggyback train nears Pulga in the Feather River Canyon, California. *Andrew Taylor*

RIGHT: WP&Y No. 7 is pictured in the dramatic landscape served by this narrow-gauge line some five miles from its destination at Whitehorse. *R. W. A. Salter*

Locomotive Types

Although the first steam locomotives operated in the U.S.—such as the *Stourbridge Lion*—were imported from Britain, it was not long before domestic production in the U.S. started. With its vast forest resources, it was inevitable that early U.S. steam locomotives would be designed as wood burners. Steam power would dominate U.S. railroads for more than a century and some of the greatest designs and developments in steam locomotive history emanated from the U.S. From the middle of the twentieth century, however, new motive power, in the form of diesel or electric locomotives, came to the forefront and by the late 1950s steam was obsolete. This section records some of the iconic designs to have emerged in almost two centuries of railroad history.

STEAM

Classic American 4-4-0

First constructed by the Norris Brothers in Philadelphia, the 4-4-0 was perhaps the epitome of the steam locomotive during the early years of railroad operation in the U.S. A total of 20,000 were built between 1840 and 1890 and, in 1870, some 85 percent of U.S. steam locomotives were of this wheel arrangement.

BELOW: A typical example of the classic American 4-4-0 is Florida Central & Peninsular Railroad No. 13. *Ian Allan Library*

RIGHT: The first steam locomotive to operate in North America came from Britain. This is a replica of one of the earliest—the *Stourbridge Lion*. *Harry Luff Collection/©Online Transport Archive*

Camel locomotives

While early U.S. steam locomotives were wood-fired, with the change to coal-firing the existing locomotive designs proved inadequate because the fireboxes had difficulty burning the anthracite coal commonly used as this time. Early coal-fired locomotives, with vertical boilers, were known as "grasshoppers" or "crabs" but these were still inadequate for the railroads' requirements. In the 1840s Ross Winans developed an alternative strategy resulting in a much-enlarged firebox and thus a smaller footplate. Known as "Camels" for self-evident reasons, the first locomotive built to Winans' design emerged in 1848. Although the design was something of a blind alleyway in the overall development of the steam engine, no fewer than 300 locomotives were built based on Winans' concept.

BELOW: One of 119 Camel locomotives operated by the Baltimore & Ohio Railroad, No. 217 of 1873 shows how this type of locomotive came to acquire its nickname. *Ian Allan Library*

Camelback or "Mother Hubbard" Locomotives

One of the most significant developments in U.S. locomotive design was the Wootten firebox, designed by John Wootten. This was an attempt to get better results in burning anthracite and required a larger grate area. The first locomotive constructed using this design emerged in 1877, but the enlarged firebox meant a reduced space for a cab. The result was a cab that straddled the boiler, with the engineer in the cab and the fireman on a small platform behind the firebox. There were a number of safety problems associated with the design and in 1918 construction of camelbacks was banned, though by this time about 3,000 examples had been built.

RIGHT: By 1918, when the ICC halted the production of camelbacks for safety reasons, no fewer than 3,000 "Mother Hubbards," such as New York Central No. 220, had been built. Three examples of the type survive in preservation. *Ian Allan Library*

Atlantic-Type Locomotives

The first Atlantic-type locomotives—4-4-2 wheel arrangement—were built for Lehigh Valley Railroad by the Vulcan Iron Works of Wilkes-Barre, Pennsylvania, in 1888. The nickname was acquired as a result of an order placed in 1894 with Baldwin Locomotive Works by Atlantic Coast Line. The design was developed with passenger service in mind, particularly shorter, high-speed runs. The Atlantics were popular with a number of railroads, though Pennsy's large fleet of 4-4-2s was probably the best known.

BELOW: The Atlantic type—exemplified by Burlington No. 1591—was designed primarily for fast passenger services. *Ian Allan Library*

RIGHT: Southern Pacific 2-8-0 No 3420 pictured at El Paso, Texas, in September 1962. *Harry Luff Collection/© Online Transport Archive*

Consolidation-Type Locomotives

The first 2-8-0 was built by Baldwin in 1866 and was named Consolidation to mark the union of the Lehigh Valley and Lehigh & Mahoney railroads. The type became the most common steam locomotive on U.S. railroads and more than 33,000 were built.

LEFT: CB&Q No. 32, one of many Consolidation-type locos operated by U.S. railroads. *Ian Allan Library Collection/© Online Transport Archive*

Prairie-Type Locomotives

The 2-6-2—or "Prairie"—was first developed to meet a need for more power than that offered by the existing Atlantic design. The first examples were built by Baldwin for export to New Zealand in 1885. While many were constructed for use in the Midwest—hence the nickname—for use on both passenger and freight services, the 2-6-2 was never common in the U.S. with the last being constructed in 1910.

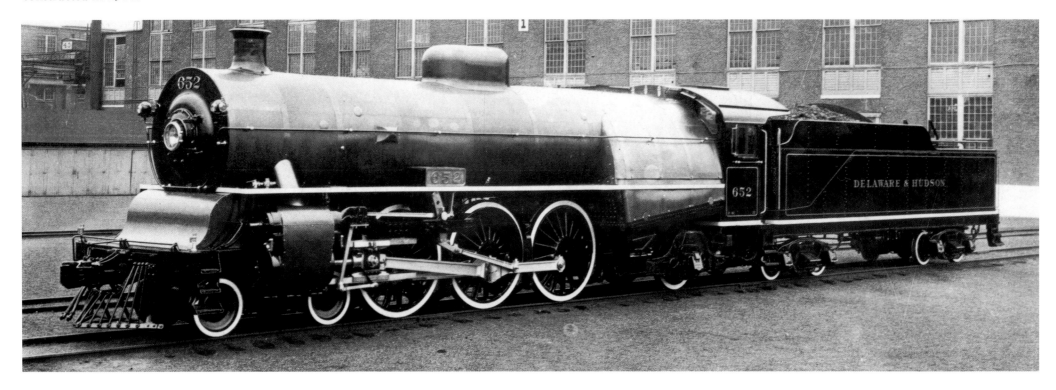

Pacific-Type Locomotives

The first 4-6-2 locomotive in the world was constructed at the Vulcan Iron Works, Wilkes-Barre, Pennsylvania, in 1886 for use on the Lehigh Valley Railroad. The first "standard" 4-6-2, as opposed to the foreshortened design built for the LVR, was constructed in 1901 by Baldwin for export to New Zealand. The wheel arrangement became a popular choice for use on express passenger services and the enlarged boiler allowed for great tractive effort than the earlier Atlantic design.

TOP: An example of a relatively uncommon wheel arrangement, the 2-6-2, was Great Northern Railway No. 1520. *Ian Allan Library*

ABOVE: A Pacific locomotive constructed for the Delaware & Hudson Railroad. *Ian Allan Library*

Pennsylvania Railroad K4 class

Among the most famous and best-performing Pacifics were Pennsy's venerable K4 class. Constructed between 1914 and 1928, a total of 425 K4s were built, 350 in the railroad's own Juniata Shops at Altoona and seventy-five by Baldwin. They were designed for use on the 131-mile-long Allegheny.

Mountain section between Altoona and Pittsburgh, where to keep the grade less than 1.7 percent, the track traversed a series of tunnels and the famous Horseshoe Curve. Throughout their life the locomotives were entrusted with the Pennsylvania Railroad's marquee trains, including the *Broadway Limited*. Two examples of the class are preserved.

ABOVE: The first of Pennsylvania Railroad's iconic K4 class, No. 1737, is pictured in 1914 shortly after its delivery from PRR's Juniata Shops at Altoona. *Ian Allan Library*

Union Pacific 9000 class

The Union Pacific Class 9000 4-12-2s were built to haul mile-long freight trains at the same speed as passenger trains. Not only were they the largest three-cylinder locomotives ever constructed, they were also the longest non-articulated locomotives ever built. When new the locomotives were largely employed on the UP main line between Cheyenne, Wyoming, and Ogden, Utah, where the route crosses the Rocky Mountains on famous Sherman Hill. Eight of the class were allocated originally to the Oregon Short Line—a subsidiary of UP—but the wheelbase was too long for that line and the locomotives passed back to UP within a year of delivery. The locomotives were replaced by the new Challenger 4-6-6-4s starting in the mid-1930s and were relegated to lesser duties; the last of the class was retired in 1956 and one example is preserved.

Hudson-Type Locomotives

The 4-6-4 locomotive was originally developed by American Locomotive Works at Schenectady, New York, for use on the New York Central Railroad and was nicknamed for the river that ran parallel to the railroad. The first of the class was constructed in 1927. The original, non-streamlined locomotives were classed "J1"—subdivided into 'a', 'b', 'c' and 'd'—and those that were streamlined were Class J3a. The four-wheel trailing truck was designed to permit a larger firebox and, by taking up water on the fly along the 960-mile route, the locomotives were able to make the New York-Chicago run in some 16 hours, with a maximum speed of 90 mph.

One of the Northern Pacific's Class Z5 2-8-8-4
locomotives, No. 5000, is pictured on the turntable at
Mandan, North Dakota, when newly delivered from
Baldwin. *Northern Pacific via Ian Allan Library*

Yellowstone-Type Locomotives

Only seventy-two Yellowstones were built, for four different railroads: B&O; Duluth, Missabe & Iron Range; NP; and SP. The first of these massive, articulated 2-8-8-4s was built by Alco for NP; it had the largest firebox ever used on a steam locomotive. Subsequent Yellowstones were built by Baldwin. The giant locomotives survived to the final years of steam, with the last of DM&IR's operating into the 1960s.

Streamlined Locomotives

In early 1934, Union Pacific unveiled the first of its streamlined diesel sets. The challenge for other railroad companies was to come up with their own version of the styling. For the New York Central it was to take an existing 4-6-4 and have it converted into streamline form. The first streamlined steam locomotive in the U.S., named Commodore Vanderbilt after the railroad's erstwhile founder, was launched later in the same year. Other railroads, such as Pennsylvania and B&O soon followed suit.

RIGHT: New York Central's 4-6-4 *Commodore Vanderbilt*. Converted to this form in 1934, this locomotive was designed for a maximum speed of 90 mph. *Ian Allan Library*

Southern Pacific Cab-Forward

Southern Pacific's 2-8-8-2 cab forward locomotives were the result of operational problems faced by the crews when working with conventional locomotives. Smoke and heat levels in the cab were intolerable because of the amount of time spent traveling through tunnels. By constructing locomotives with cabs at the front and by adopting oil-firing, crew working conditions improved.

BELOW LEFT: Southern Pacific's No. 4133 was typical of the railroad's cab-forward design locomotives. *Ian Allan Library*

Union Pacific 800-class Northerns

Union Pacific's forty-five 800-class 4-8-4 locomotives were constructed between 1937 and 1944. They were the world's first 4-8-4 designed to haul passenger trains at speeds in excess of 90 mph. During 1938 one of the class, No. 815, achieved a speed of 102.4 mph and sustained speeds in excess of 100 mph for six miles. The Northerns were popular with several railroads—thirty-six carriers operated more than 1,100 of the locomotives—and were actually nicknamed for Northern Pacific. But, few are better known and loved as much as UP's, thanks to preserved No. 844, which still makes periodic trips to the delight of U.S. steam fans.

BELOW: Union Pacific No. 802 was typical of the railroad's first batch of 4-8-4 locomotives. *Ian Allan Library*

Berkshire-Type Locomotives

Developed by the Lima Locomotive Works of Lima, Ohio, the first 2-8-4s were built for the Boston & Albany Railroad for use on its line in the Berkshire Mountains—hence the nickname. Often regarded as the epitome of steam "super power," examples of the type were supplied to a number of railroads by both Lima and Baldwin.

BELOW: Chesapeake & Ohio was a major user of Berkshire locomotives, as exemplified by No. 2744; sister locomotive No. 2716 is preserved. *Ian Allan Library*

RIGHT: Another railroad to use 4-8-4s was the Reading; here tow of that railroad's Class T-1 are pictured running in tandem at Weigh Scales, Pennsylvania, alongside Pa Route #61 in late 1963. *Harry Luff Collection/© Online Transport Archive*

Norfolk & Western Class J 4-8-4

Norfolk & Western's Class J 4-8-4 was the last American steam locomotive designed specifically for express passenger service . The first of the class was built at the railroad's Roanoke, Virginia, shops and completed in early 1941.

Ultimately, a total of fourteen were built; when No. 613 was finished in 1950 it became the last new steam passenger locomotive built in the U.S. Highly successful in service, the locomotives operated some 80 percent of the railroad's passenger services until supplanted later in the 1950s. One of the locomotives, No. 611, has been preserved.

BELOW: Norfolk & Western No. 600 was the first of the railroad's 14-strong Class J 4-8-4s, which represented the ultimate in U.S. steam passenger locomotive design. *Ian Allan Library*

"Big Boys"

Constructed by Alco between 1941 and 1944, the twenty-five members of Union Pacific's class of 4-8-8-4 locomotives were regarded as the most powerful steam locomotives ever built. Constructed to haul freight trains over UP's high-altitude main line in Wyoming and Utah, the giant articulated locomotives—nicknamed "Big Boys"—were capable of hauling some 500 tons of freight at speeds of up to 80 mph. To operate the locomotives the railroad constructed the world's largest turntables, 135 feet in diameter, at Green River, Wyoming, and Ogden, Utah. Though few were built, the Big Boys are well represented in preservation with no fewer than eight examples having escaped the scrapyard.

RIGHT: One of UP's twenty-five Big Boys, No. X4014, is seen about to enter the tunnel at Hermosa, Wyoming, during the summer of 1955. *W. H. N. Rossiter*

OPPOSITE, ABOVE: A 900hp diesel locomotive supplied to the New York Central Railroad in 1928 for use on passenger trains. *Ian Allan Library*

OPPOSITE, BELOW: The first General Motors FT locomotives emerged from the new La Grange, Illinois, factory in 1938. Among customers for this widely used type was Union Pacific. *Union Pacific*

DIESEL

The invention of diesel internal-combustion engine by the German Rudolf Diesel at the end of the 19th century was ultimately to spell the end of steam. Using oil, rather than gasoline, the diesel engine was cheaper to fuel but the early designs were too cumbersome to be used in locomotives and it was not until the 1920s that the first practical diesel-electric — where the diesel engine powers a generator which in turn creates electricity to drive the train — locomotive. The major break through came as a result of research by General Motors, led by Charles Kettering, which used lightweight alloys to improve yet further the power/weight ratio. In the late 1930s GM's Electro-Motive Division — EMD — constructed a new plant at La Grange, Illinois, for the construction of diesel locomotives; the revolution had begun in earnest. Other US manufacturers, such as Alco, followed suit and vast number of a variety of diesel designs soon began to emerge.

BELOW: An Amtrak SDP40F locomotive is pictured in the outskirts of Boston with a Boston–New York train in 1974. *Brian J. Cuddahy*

RIGHT: An SD60M constructed by the EMD of General Motors for use by Union Pacific. *Ian Allan Library*

ABOVE: Penn Central EMD No. 4305 with the *Juniata* pictured at Horseshoe Curve, Altoona, Pennsylvania. In the distance can be seen preserved Pennsylvania Railroad 4-6-2 No. 1361. *H. Bongaardt*

RIGHT: An Alco-built DL-721 belonging to San Diego & Eastern Arizona Railroad. *P. R. Parr*

LEFT: The diesel-powered RDC produced by Budd was designed for low-cost passenger services. *Harry Luff Collection/© Online Transport Archive*

ABOVE: Pictured at Miami, Seaboard System No. 2138 is an SD40 produced by GM. *Harry Luff Collection/© Online Transport Archive*

LEFT: Amtrak service #303 from Chicago to St Louis seen at Springfield, Illinois, *Harry Luff Collection/© Online Transport Archive*

ABOVE: During the summer of 1979 Rock Island Railroad service #301 pictured at Blue Island with a local formed of double-deck coaching stock. *Harry Luff Collection/© Online Transport Archive*

RIGHT: The *Olympian Hiawatha* was one of the Chicago, Milwaukee, St. Paul & Pacific Railroad's most important services and, in 1947, the service was provided with new streamlined coaches, including the stylish "Skytop Lounge" observation cars, as seen here. *Harry Luff Collection/© Online Transport Archive*

LEFT: Two Conrail diesel locomotives power a freight through Puritas Rapid station. *Harry Luff Collection/© Online Transport Archive*

ABOVE: Constructed by GM between 1956 and 1960, the "FL9" was a passenger version of a predominantly freight model; two of the class, belonging to Penn Central, are seen at either end of the single-coach Dover Plains shuttle at Dover Plains. *Harry Luff Collection/© Online Transport Archive*

RIGHT: Southern Pacific Class SD9 No. 4374 was an EMD product of the mid-1950s; it was withdrawn before the SP and UP merged in 1996 although a number of the type did survive briefly in the expanded UP's ownership. *Harry Luff Collection/© Online Transport Archive*

ELECTRIC

Alongside the diesel engine, electric power also offered a major challenge to steam's supremacy; indeed practical electric locomotives predated the invention of the internal combustion engine. With no pollution directly produced, electric traction was an attractive option in areas—such a long tunnels—where ventilation was a problem. The first line in the U.S. to use electric traction was the Baltimore & Ohio in 1895 when a 3.75-mile long line in Baltimore was electrified in order to circumvent the city's ban on smoke from locomotives. Further systems soon followed, adopting both AC and DC power; the former was better for long-distance whilst the latter was cheaper and well-suited for intensive commuter lines. The Great Northern electrified its line through the Cascade Tunnels from 1909; however, the Great

Northern removed the electrification in 1956 when the line was converted to diesel-electric operation. Another line that was converted to electric traction was the Chicago, Milwaukee, St. Paul & Pacific Railroad which began converting its 900-mile route from St Paul to Seattle in 1914. Using hydro-electric power and massive bi-polar locomotives —nicknamed "Little Joes" (after Joseph Stalin because the locomotives were embargoed before export to the USSR)— this was another line that succumbed to diesel traction after World War 2. Electric traction remains around many major U.S. cities as the power behind the essential commuter networks and also on a limited number of long-distance routes such as that from New York to Washington via Philadelphia.

LEFT: One of the New York Central T class B-B+B-B locomotives, introduced in 1913, No. 1166 is pictured at the head of a passenger train. The NYC lines were electrified after an accident in 1902 that killed fifteen passengers caused by an engineer missing a red signal obscured by smoke. The line was electrified at 650V dc using a third rail and these locomotives were unusual in that they possessed gearless drives, with the motors being mounted directly on the axles. *New York Central via Ian Allan Library*

RIGHT: Constructed from 1975, the GE-built E-60CP class of electric locomotive were designed by Amtrak to replace the GG1s. Although, at 6,000 hp, they were, at that date, the most powerful locomotives in the U.S., they failed to be reliable at the speeds intended—125 mph—and Amtrak looked to France for its next generation of electric locomotive. *Harry Luff Collection/© Online Transport Archive*

LEFT: Constructed by General Electric in the late 1920s for the Great Northern Railroad, No. 5012 was designed to operate at 11kV ac. The locomotive weighed an impressive 259 tons. *GE via Ian Allan Library*

RIGHT: Still looking good despite being forty years old, two of the Pennsylvania Railroad's stylish GG1 electric locomotives double-head a freight. The last of the locomotives were retired from mainline service in 1983, bringing to an end the operation of Raymond Loewy-designed locomotives on U.S. railroads. *Albert Kruger*

BELOW: Constructed by General Electric, No. 7809, one of the L5 class, was delivered to the Pennsylvania Railroad in the early 1920s. Built to operate over lines electrified with a third rail, the locomotives were also fitted with pantographs to operate over those sections where overhead was installed. *GE via Ian Allan Library*

LEFT: The first of the GG1 class of electric locomotives, No 4800, was repainted in a special commemorative livery to mark the bicentenary of the Declaration of Independence in 1976. *Harry Luff Collection/© Online Transport Archive*

ABOVE: New Haven Railroad No 374, an EP-5-class locomotive, pictured at New Haven, Connecticut. *Harry Luff Collection/© Online Transport Archive*

ABOVE: A line-up of classic Pennsylvania Railroad electric locomotives at Altoona, Pennsylvania, in the early 1960s. *Harry Luff Collection/© Online Transport Archive*

RIGHT: A rake of New York, New Haven & Hartford Railroad Class EF4 electric locomotives haul a freight near Bay Ridge, Long Island. *Harry Luff Collection/© Online Transport Archive*

Railroad Preservation

Almost from the dawn of the railroad age promoters realized that there was considerable commercial potential in constructing lines specifically for tourists. In 1869 the Mount Washington cog railway opened; other examples of tourist-oriented routes included Santa Fe's Grand Canyon Railway and the Georgetown Loop. However, just as the major railroads suffered from the rise of the internal combustion engine, so too did many of these pioneering tourist railways and, with exceptions (such as the Mount Washington line), the majority fell by the wayside. This was not, necessarily, the end of the story because many of these lines have been resurrected in some cases, ironically, as a means of reducing the pressure on tourist sites caused by road traffic. A notable example of this is the Grand Canyon line, which originally closed in 1968, but which was reopened in 1991.

The first standard gauge preserved line in the world was the Strasburg Rail Road in Pennsylvania. The world's second railroad to receive a charter (only the Ffestiniog Railway in Wales beat it by two weeks), which it obtained on June 9, 1832, the Strasburg Railroad provided a link ultimately between Strasburg and the main New York-Chicago line at Leaman Place. Freight only from 1920, the line closed completely in 1958. However, having been purchased by Henry K. Long, it reopened the following year and now has been carrying passengers as a tourist line for almost half a century. When the 4.5-mile line was originally reopened it was initially as a freight line, with limited passenger service, but while revenue on freight was below expectations, earnings on the passenger side were encouraging enough to suggest that the company concentrate on this aspect. Where the Strasburg blazed a trail, other lines both in the U.S. and throughout the world have followed.

LEFT: GWR 2-10-0 No. 90 pictured at Goff's on the Strasburg Railroad, Pennsylvania, on August 23, 1973. *Ian Allan Library*

ABOVE: The Mount Washington Cog Railway remains operational as a tourist line. The unusual arrangement of boiler is designed to ensure that it remains level during the ascent and descent of the mountain. *Corbis*

In many respects the Strasburg Rail Road's preservation is very typical of North America. Unlike Europe, where many preservation schemes were not developed from any particular commercial aspiration but from a desire to preserve something that was in danger of being lost, the U.S. is more oriented towards the commercial tourist market. While there are conventional museums—such as the Baltimore & Ohio Railroad Museum and the Smithsonian—these are atypical. While most European countries have state-sponsored national railroad museums—such as Britain's National Railway Museum in York—covering the entire country's railroad history there is nothing directly comparable in the U.S. Moreover, while the majority of preserved lines in Europe are staffed almost exclusively with volunteers with relatively few paid staff, in the U.S. the reverse is true.

As part of the tourist industry there is an element of show business in many of the U.S.'s "preserved" lines. A notable example of this is the three-mile-long Tweetsie Railroad, near Blowing Rock, North Carolina. Closer in concept to a theme park, the trains are held up by "bandits" and attacked by "Indians" before returning passengers to Tweetsie Town where a typical railroad town of the end of the nineteenth century has been faithfully reconstructed.

While examples of many of the most important designs of steam locomotive had survived—including no fewer than eight of the class Union Pacific "Big Boys"—there are also countless examples of classic designs that have not survived. Among the many losses are New York Central's streamlined J3 class Hudsons and iconic Niagara 4-8-4s. Although efforts were made preserve at least one example of the former, prevailing attitudes in the period were such that the efforts

RIGHT: A single unit ascends the Manitou & Pikes Peak Railway; the view shows the center, cogged, track that allows locomotives and rolling stock to ascend and descend steep grades safely. *Harry Luff Collection/Online Transport Archive*

FAR RIGHT: Ex-Chicago, Burlington & Quincy No. 5629 preserved at the Colorado Railroad Museum. *Harry Luff Collection/Online Transport Archive*

failed. Two members of the Smithsonian Institute approached NYC to acquire an example in the mid-1950s, only to have their request rejected by the company's president, S. J. Pearlman. Like many of his contemporaries, Pearlman believed that steam was obsolete and that, on retirement, the locomotives should be consigned to the scrapyard.

The strength of the preservation movement is that it is a nationwide phenomenon. There are examples of museums across the country, from the Baltmore & Ohio Museum in Baltimore to the California State Railroad Museum. There are also countless preserved lines, both standard and narrow gauge, offering tourists the opportunity of sampling railroad travel as it existed in the past. But preservation is more than simply locomotives and rolling stock; it also involves the conservation of historical artifacts—from tickets to timetables and from signals to stationery. These are not the most glamorous parts of the nation's railway heritage, but without their conservation future generations will not be able fully to appreciate the U.S.'s rich railroad history.

Moreover, it's a history that moves forward day by day; just as the steam locomotive was deemed outmoded in the 1950s, so more recent locomotives and rolling stock are also gradually becoming obsolete. The original EMD diesels are now as much a part of history as the steam locomotives they were destined to replace and many examples of these types of rolling stock are also finding their way into museum collections.

It's not just the preservationists that have realized that money can be made from running special trains. Increasingly, railroad companies themselves have realized that money can be made from running special trains aimed at tourists. A notable example of this is the Arcade & Attica Railroad in New York State; the railroad initially withdrew all passenger services in 1951, but reintroduced a steam train in 1962. Such has been the success of the train over the 7.5 miles between Arcade and Curriers that the company now runs a regular tourist service each summer. Another mainline company that operated steam specials was the Southern Railway, which employed three steam locomotives for a number of years. Two of these were 2-8-0s built originally for the company but sold

when steam was retired, before being reacquired for these services. A third 2-8-0 was loaned by the Tennessee Valley Railroad Museum. With the merger of Southern and Norfolk & Western in 1982 the newly enlarged company expanded its steam operations, restoring the classic Norfolk & Western Class J 4-8-4 No. 611 to service.

In a sense, with the realization by railroad companies that money can be made from these services, preservation has come full circle. Initially designed to secure historical items that were considered spent by the railroads, the railroads have now come to realize that such assets can be used to bring in additional revenue.

LEFT: Denver & Rio Grande No. 473 switches cars after the completion of a day's work. *P. T. Nunn*

ABOVE: A diesel-hauled train in the autumn forest: a Conway Scenic Railroad train near the White Mountains in 2005. *Franz-Marc Frei/Corbis*

ABOVE: Captured at Steamtown in July 1981, No. 519 was originally operated by the Maine Central Railroad. *Harry Luff Collection/Online Transport Archive*

RIGHT: Ex- Gulf, Mobile & Northern 4-6-2 No. 425 pictured at Kimberton, Pennsylvania, on the Valley Forge Scenic Railroad. *H. Bongaardt*

PAGE 178: A gold star decorates the bright red hub of a locomotive wheel at the State Railroad Museum in Sacramento, California. *Stephanie Maze/Corbis*

PAGE 179: Cumbres and Toltec Scenic Railroad—a 64-mile, fully operational steam railroad jointly owned by the states of Colorado and New Mexico. *Macduff Everton/Corbis*

LEFT: Wilmington & Western 2-6-0 No. 92 recorded during a run from Greenbank to Mount Cuba, Delaware. *H. Bongaardt*

ABOVE: Located on Maui Island, Hawaii, the Lahaina, Kaanapali & Pacific Railroad runs for some four miles. Known as the "Sugar Cane Railway" it now carries tourists through the sugar cane fields that led to railway development on the island. *Corbis*

LEFT: A replica of Union Pacific No. 119 preserved at Promontory Point, Utah, at the point at which the golden spike was hammered into place to celebrate completion of America's first transcontinental railroad. *P. J. Howard*

ABOVE: Cumbres and Toltec Scenic Railroad steam train in Chama, New Mexico. *Jonathan Blair/Corbis*

ABOVE: Carrying visitors on an extended tour of the region, steam locomotives of the Durango and Silverton Narrow Gauge Railroad make a stop in the old mining town of Durango, Colorado. *Lowell Georgia/Corbis*

RIGHT: The Durango and Silverton Narrow Gauge Railroad steam train arrives in Silverton, Colorado. *Lowell Georgia/Corbis*

LEFT: Classic diesel engine No. 573 at the Conway Scenic Railroad Depot in North Conway, New Hampshire. *Lee Snider/Photo Images/Corbis*

ABOVE: A steam engine sits by the wooden railroad station in Old Tucson. The train gives short rides to tourists. Old Tucson was built as a movie set. It has been expanded and is now a tourist attraction. *Buddy Mays/Corbis*

LEFT: A steam locomotive for the Durango and Silverton Narrow Gauge Railroad. Durango, Colorado. *Buddy Mays/Corbis*

ABOVE: The historic Grand Canyon Railroad. The train runs from Williams, Arizona to Grand Canyon Village on the North Rim of the canyon. *Buddy Mays/Corbis*

ABOVE: Pine Creek Railroad 3-foot-gauge Shay No. 6 on display in Allaire State Park, New Jersey. *H. Bongaardt*

RIGHT: *Sequioa* and *Fern* outside the roundhouse on the Redwood Valley Railway, near San Francisco, California. *Ian Allan Library*

Abbreviations

Alco	American Locomotive Works
AT&SF	Atchison, Topeka & Santa Fe Railway
B&M	Boston & Maine Railroad
B&O	Baltimore & Ohio Railroad
BNSF	Burlington Northern Santa Fe Railroad
C&O	Chesapeake & Ohio Railroad
CB&Q	Chicago, Burlington & Quincy Railroad
CMStP&P	Chicago, Milwaukee, St. Paul & Pacific Railroad

C&NW	Chicago & North Western Railroad
DM&IR	Duluth, Missabe & Iron Range Railroad
EMD	Electro-Motive Division of General Motors
GE	General Electric
GMO	Gulf, Mobile and Ohio Railroad
GN	Great Northern Railroad
IC	Illinois Central Railroad
ICC	Interstate Commerce Commission
MEC	Maine Central Railroad
NP	Northern Pacific Railroad

N&W	Norfolk & Western Railroad
NYC	New York Central Railroad
PRR	Pennsylvania Railroad or "Pennsy"
RDC	Rail diesel car
SD&AE	San Diego & Easteran Arizona Railroad
SP	Southern Pacific Railroad
UP	Union Pacific Railroad
WP&Y	White Pass & Yukon Railroad

RIGHT: A fireman shovels coal into the furnace of a steam locomotive at the Frostburg Railroad Station in Frostburg, Maryland. The Western Maryland Scenic Railroad locomotive, built in 1916, hauls passengers in refurbished cars through western Maryland's Allegheny Mountains from Cumberland to Frostburg, a trip of about 11 miles. *Paul A. Souders/Corbis*